edexcel
advancing learning, changing lives

Literacy

Level 2

A PEARSON COMPANY

Esther Menon

Consultants **Geoff Barton and Muriel Lloyd Lavery**

Contents

About this Skills Book

This book is designed to help you develop your skills in reading, writing, spelling, punctuation and grammar. These skills are very important in everyday life, and having a greater understanding of them should increase your confidence, help you to fulfil your potential, and give you more control over what you choose to do with your life. Achieving a Level 2 qualification in Adult Literacy will prove that you have developed your knowledge and skills to this standard.

This Skills Book will help you to pass the Level 2 Adult Literacy test by helping you develop exactly those skills that you need for the test. This means that you'll take the test feeling more comfortable and more confident that you can succeed. Here's how:

- **Section A: Reading for information and understanding**
  Develop different reading skills by scanning for key words, skimming to work out what a text is about, reading in detail and finding the main points.

- **Section B: Understanding the features of different texts**
  Learn about how information is organised in texts. Understand how to read tables using words, symbols and numbers.

- **Section C: Understanding how writers achieve their purpose**
  Find out about the different ways in which texts are written in order to describe, explain, persuade and argue, and the differences between formal and informal texts.

- **Section D: Spelling words correctly**
  Get lots of tips for improving your spelling plus plenty of practice in spotting and correcting spelling mistakes.

- **Section E: Using punctuation correctly**
  Practise punctuating sentences, using commas, apostrophes, inverted commas and paragraphs.

- **Section F: Using good grammar**
  Learn to spot and solve common problems with grammar, such as connecting parts of a sentence, getting verb tenses right, making sure the subject and verb of a sentence agree, and using pronouns.

- **Section G: Preparing for the test**
  Finally pull all your skills together and make sure you are ready for the test, with guidance on and practice at reading and answering the different types of question.

How to use this book

Each section starts with a short explanation, followed by a wide range of activities to help you understand the skill. Each section ends with a short test, and you can record your scores in the chart at the back of this book to see your own progress.

Most people find some of the skills easier to master than others, and the Teacher's Handbook has practice sheets to go with each skill so you get plenty of support with anything you find difficult. This symbol 24 at the end of each section tells you which pages of the Teacher's Handbook to refer to. There is also a Hot Topics CD-ROM with games to help you enjoy practising your skills, and your teacher will have a Practice Tests CD-ROM to help you revise for the test.

It's as simple as that. Get ready to feel your confidence improve. Good luck and enjoy developing new skills.

A Reading for information and understanding

This section will help you to practise different ways of reading to obtain information from texts. You will learn about:

▷▷ skimming, scanning and close reading

▷▷ understanding difficult words

▷▷ finding main points and details.

You will then test your mastery of these skills at the end of the section.

1 Skimming, scanning and close reading

⏸ First read this ...

When you read a piece of text, you often need to use all three of these skills to find out the information you need.

■ **Skimming** means looking over a text quickly to find out what it's about.

■ **Scanning** means quickly running your eyes across the page to find the answer to a particular question.

■ **Close reading** means reading a text carefully so you can really understand it.

▶▶ Now try it!

1 Look at the article on page 5, from the sports pages in an online newspaper. Answer the questions below.

a) **Skim** the article to find out what it is about. You will need to look at the heading and photo, and run your eye down the text looking for words that tell you which sport it is about.

Which sport is the text about? Tick the right answer.

A Bowling ☐

B Baseball ☐

C Cricket ☐

D Football ☐

b) **Scan** the text to find out whether Monty Panesar is left-handed or right-handed. (Circle) the words in the text that tell you this.

c) **Read the text closely** to find out what Monty Panesar thinks about Sachin Tendulkar. <u>Underline</u> the words that tell you Monty Panesar thinks Sachin Tendulkar is a great cricketer.

d) **Scan the text** and then **read a paragraph closely** to find out which other players Monty defeated as well as Sachin Tendulkar, in the same match. Write the other players' names here:

_____ .

e) **Read closely** and then (circle) the words that tell you in which match in the tour Monty defeated all three players.

Sports**News**

Front Page
Home News
World News
Health News
Earth News
Science News
▶Sport News
Timeout
Mailbag
Competitions
Conservation
Subscriptions
Parents
Teachers
Contact Us

New England spin doctor!

If a bowler in cricket were asked to name a batsman he would like to dismiss on his Test match debut, he would struggle to name
5 a better player than India's Sachin Tendulkar.

Known as the Little Master, he has struck more than 10,000 runs, averages more than 55 per innings
10 and has smashed 35 centuries. Bowling to him is enough to make most youngsters shake with fear.

However, Monty Panesar, Northamptonshire's left-arm
15 spinner, who is just 23, showed his character by trapping his hero lbw during England's recent tour of India.

He also removed Mohammad Kaif
20 and, in the second innings, skipper Rahul Dravid, to round off a highly promising first match.

'Everyone dreams of getting [Sachin's] wicket,' said Panesar,
25 who has been nicknamed the Turbanator. 'To get someone like him, my role model and the best batsman in the world, is something special.'

2 Answer the questions below. They go with the text on page 7.

a) **Skim** the text opposite. What kind of text is it?

A A persuasive text to encourage readers to support Charlton women's football team. ☐

B A newspaper article about women's football. ☐

C A newspaper article about the footballer Eniola Aluko. ☐

D An explanation text explaining how to become a football player. ☐

b) **Scan** the text to find out which team Eniola Aluko scored her first goal for England against.

A Holland ☐

B Czech Republic ☐

C Everton ☐

D Charlton ☐

c) **Scan** the text to find out what subject Eniola Aluko is studying at university.

A Sport ☐

B Politics ☐

C Media ☐

D Law ☐

d) **Skim** to find the part of the text where Eniola Aluko is talking about her brother. **Read closely** to find out what she thinks of him.

A She thinks he's a great player. ☐

B She's a bit jealous of him. ☐

C She doesn't often manage to see him play. ☐

D She tries to play on the same days as him. ☐

e) **Skim** to find the part of the text where Eniola is talking about her studies. **Read closely** to find out what she thinks about combining football with studying.

A It's easy because she knows a lot about the subject. ☐

B It's important to study because she will need a job if her football career ends early. ☐

C It's too difficult and stressful. ☐

D It's difficult, but her father can help her. ☐

Test tip!

It is often a good idea to read the questions before you read the text. That way, you'll know what to look out for when you read the text and which reading skills to use.

Test tip!

Close reading is very important. It will help you to understand the text more fully and you will be more confident that you are answering the question asked. Take time to read important areas of text several times until you feel you really understand them.

Sports **News**

Front Page
Home News
World News
Health News
Earth News
Science News
▶Sport News
Timeout
Mailbag
Competitions
Conservation
Subscriptions
Parents
Teachers
Contact Us

Real-life star's World Cup ambitions

England star Eniola Aluko was named Young Player of the Year at the Women's FA Awards three years ago and since then she hasn't looked back.

5 The 19-year-old striker has played for England Under-19s and 21s and made her debut for the senior side against Holland in a 2–1 win two years ago.

Last May, against the Czech Republic, she
10 scored her first goal for England, and she also scored the only goal in the FA Women's Cup final for Charlton against Everton at Upton Park, in a game shown live on BBC One.

This season she scored twice for Charlton in
15 the 2–1 League Cup victory over Arsenal.

She studies law at Brunel University and her brother Sone plays for Birmingham and England Under 17s. Eniola is going places.

She spoke to The Newspaper:

20 **You play for Charlton – are they a top women's side?**

Courtesy of the FA

During the past four years Charlton have reached a number of major finals and have won at least one trophy each season. I support the men's team as well because we're all part of the same club. The women's team is
25 equally important to the club's vision and we're given space in matchday programmes.

You're studying law: how do you find the time?

Juggling law and football is extremely hard and stressful at times, but it's something I have to do to make sure I have something to fall back on if my playing career ends early. Law is something that's always interested me. My father was a member of parliament in Nigeria so
30 I know quite a lot about law and politics. I hope to work in sports law, media law or human-rights law.

How thrilling was it for you to score your first England goal against the Czech Republic at Walsall in May 2005?

I was delighted because it was my first senior goal and it rounded off a good performance
35 by the team leading up to last year's European Championships.

Is there a big rivalry between you and Sone?

No, he's a fantastic player who can use both feet – that is quite rare. I admire him and try to emulate his skills. We're very happy for each other when we score. We try to see each other play but sometimes we play on the same days.

2 Understanding difficult words

First read this ...

When you need to work out what a word means, you can:

■ stop when you read the word that you need to understand.

■ ask yourself these questions:

1 What is the rest of the sentence or paragraph about?

2 Can I break down the word to find any smaller words I know?

3 Do I know any other words that look like this word?

4 Is it a word with more than one meaning? If so, which of the meanings makes sense?

Now try it!

1 a) If you don't know the meaning of 'yielding', you can work it out by **looking at the rest of the sentence**:

He grabbed a spade and dug easily into the **yielding** ground.

b) Work out the meaning of 'hastily' by looking at the rest of the sentence. Tick the word that could best be used in place of 'hastily'.

She drove **hastily** around the narrow country lanes, so she got to the party on time.

A carelessly ☐

B dangerously ☐

C quickly ☐

D carefully ☐

I think yielding means something like soft. The ground must have been soft if he could dig easily.

2 a) If you don't know the meaning of 'multiracial', you can **break it down into smaller parts**.

We can describe Britain as a **multiracial** society.

b) Work out the meaning of 'misshapen' by breaking the word down. Tick the word or words that could best be used in place of 'misshapen'.

The **misshapen** tin of soup was 10p cheaper than the other tins.

A oddly shaped ☐

B unlucky ☐

C inexpensive ☐

D out of date ☐

Multi means lots of. Racial means something about races. So multiracial probably means lots of people from different races all living together.

3 a) If you don't know what 'purify' means, you can think of **other words you know that look like it.**

> To **purify** the muddy water he poured it through filter paper.

> *Pure* can mean **clean**. To **purify** the muddy water probably means to **clean** the muddy water.

b) Work out the meaning of the word 'desensitise' by thinking about other words that are like it. Tick the words that could best be used in place of 'desensitise the skin' in this sentence:

> The nurse used a cream to **desensitise** the skin before the injection.

A clean the skin ☐

B push the skin down ☐

C make the skin less sensitive ☐

D prepare the skin ☐

4 a) If you don't know what 'medium' means in this sentence, you can **look it up in the dictionary.**

> The **medium** stared at the people around the table.

> In this sentence 'a person who claims they can talk to the dead' is the only meaning that makes sense.

The dictionary might say:

Medium. *adj.* **1.** middle. **2** average. **3** person who claims they can talk to the dead.

b) Use a dictionary to work out the meaning of 'ensure' in the sentence:

> I will **ensure** that you are happy with the finished job.

Tick the sentence that means the same as the sentence above.

A I will pay you some money if you are not happy with the finished job. ☐

B I will make sure you are happy with the finished job. ☐

C I am sure that you are happy with the finished job. ☐

D I hope you will be happy with the finished job. ☐

Test tip!

When you need to think of the meaning of a particular word or choose a word to replace one in the text, make sure you understand how the word is being used in the context of the text.

3 Finding main points and details

First read this ...

- **The main point** in a piece of text is what the text is mostly about. You may need to find the main point of a whole text, or the main point of one paragraph or section.

- Paragraphs or sections will often begin with one main point. The main point is often followed by examples and **details** that add extra information to the main point.

- Sometimes the main point does not come first in the paragraph – then you may have to read the whole section carefully to find the main point.

- You need to be able to tell the difference between a main point and a detail.

Now try it!

Look at the information below, which was written for people thinking about becoming firefighters. Then answer the questions on page 11.

The main point in the first paragraph has been highlighted in red. The detail has been highlighted in green.

Dealing with emergencies

Technology obviously plays a major role in helping firefighters to tackle emergencies as efficiently as possible. For example, at brigade headquarters control room computers store street plans, details of high risk buildings and the latest information on hazardous materials. This ensures that as soon as
5 an emergency call is received – whether a fire, chemical spillage or road traffic accident – controllers can immediately access what appliances are required.

On attending at a fire, the firefighters have to make a very quick assessment of the situation. As materials used in homes and factories
10 change so does the way a fire is tackled. A house fire may require two appliances whereas a commercial or factory fire may involve several appliances as well as requiring thousands of litres of water and foam, plus the use of specialist equipment.

There is also the hazard of toxic fumes and heavy smoke which can be
15 generated from the modern materials – for example foam-filled furniture. This makes tackling a fire that much more difficult and firefighters always go fully protected with equipment such as breathing apparatus as well as personal radio sets to keep them in contact with their colleagues at the scene, or back at brigade headquarters.

1 a) Draw a <u>wavy line</u> under the main points in paragraphs 2 and 3.

Circle the detail in paragraphs 2 and 3. (Phrases such as 'for example' and 'as in the case of' often suggest that details will follow.)

b) Tick the sentence that best summarises the main point in paragraph 2.

A When they arrive at a fire, firefighters need to work out quickly what equipment they need. ☐

B Factory fires need more equipment than house fires. ☐

C Fighting fires uses up a great deal of water. ☐

D Firefighters have a lot of specialist equipment. ☐

c) Summarise the main point made in paragraph 3 in your own words.

_____

_____

_____

_____

_____

_____

d) Which of the following headings would be most suitable to use as a heading for the second paragraph?

A Materials used in homes and factories ☐

B Using specialist equipment ☐

C How firefighters decide how to tackle a fire ☐

D When a fire starts ☐

e) Which of the following does the text say is a danger caused by modern materials?

A Toxic fumes. ☐

B Heavy use of water and foam. ☐

C Chemical spillage. ☐

D Road traffic accidents. ☐

f) Which of the following would make the best alternative heading for the whole passage?

A What to do if you discover a fire ☐

B Why join the fire service? ☐

C Fighting a factory fire ☐

D Firefighting equipment ☐

Test tip!

In the test it is a good idea to read important parts of the text several times to check that you have noticed and understood everything you need to answer the question.

2 Read this karate instructor profile from the Karate Union of Great Britain website, and answer the questions.

Sensei Billy Higgins 7th Dan

Billy Higgins was born in Bootle, Liverpool on 14th August 1945. His sporting skills have been clear from a young age. Taking a keen interest in sport from an early age, he took up boxing, gymnastics, and football while still at school. In 1965 he started to study Wado Ryu Karate and he very quickly established himself as a fast and skilful fighter.

He moved to KUGB from the BKCC in 1970. He was selected for the BKCC All Styles Squad and during training, he rapidly realised the high technical standard of the KUGB members of the squad.

He has had a long and distinguished competition career, with many national and international titles to his credit. These include Individual 2nd in the WUKO All Styles World Championship in Paris 1975 and 1976 European All Styles Champion. He was captain of the highly successful 1975 British All Styles team that defeated the Japanese team to win the World Championships in Los Angeles. He was also a member of the very successful KUGB Senior International Team that won the Championships of Europe no less than five times!

He has had a range of regional and national responsibilities. He was coach and manager of the EKB squad and was squad coach for the KUGB Scottish and Southern Regions. He is a KUGB Grading Examiner and a qualified International Referee.

He is renowned for his fast and effective fighting style, particularly his lightning-fast Ashi-Barai/Gyaku-Tsuki combination which has devastated his opponents and won him many events.

a) <u>Underline</u> the main point of the third paragraph.

b) Which of the following would be the best title for the first paragraph?

   A Early sporting interests ☐

   B Billy's birth ☐

   C Billy's school career ☐

   D Studying Wado Ryu Karate ☐

c) Fill in the table below by summarising the main points of each paragraph in your own words.

Paragraph	Main point
1	Billy Higgins has always been good at sport.
2	He moved from the BKCC to the KUGB.
3	
4	
5	

d) What role did Billy play in the team that won the 1975 World Championships?

_____

e) Work out from the passage which of the following best describes the Ashi-Barai/Gyaku-Tsuki combination:

   A Specialist equipment that you need for karate. ☐

   B Specialist clothing that you need for karate. ☐

   C A medal you can get for winning karate competitions. ☐

   D Fighting moves you can use in karate. ☐

Test tip

When a question asks you to choose a statement that **best sums up** what a paragraph or text is about, you need to work out what the main point of the text is.

f) Circle two phrases in the text that describe Billy Higgins' fighting style.

g) Which of the following is **not** true of Billy Higgins, according to the text?

   A He joined the BKCC in 1970. ☐

   B He is a qualified referee. ☐

   C He has captained the British karate team. ☐

   D He played football when he was young. ☐

4 Test your skills

Use the test below to find out how well you have mastered the skills in Section A.

To complete this test you will need to use your skimming, scanning and close reading skills. You will also need to work out the meanings of words, and identify main points and details in the text.

These questions are all about the text opposite.

1   Which of the following best describes the main purpose of this text?

A ☐   To give general information about Rastafarianism.

B ☐   To persuade people to become Rastafarians.

C ☐   To explain the history of Rastafarianism.

D ☐   To argue that the Rastafarian lifestyle is a good one.

2   In which country did Rastafarianism start?

A ☐   Egypt

B ☐   Ethiopia

C ☐   Jamaica

D ☐   Israel

3   Which of the following words could best replace the word 'compelling' on line 27?

A ☐   annoying

B ☐   likeable

C ☐   attractive

D ☐   enjoyable

4   Which of the following would be the best heading to use on line 8?

A ☐   The African roots of Rastafarianism

B ☐   What do Rastafarians believe?

C ☐   Rastafarians' hopes for the future

D ☐   Why is Ethiopia important to Rastafarians?

5   Why did Jamaican Rastafarians originally develop reggae music?

A ☐   To spread their religion.

B ☐   To express their thoughts.

C ☐   To gain fame all over the world.

D ☐   To worship God.

6 Which of the following is **not** an aspect of Rastafarian beliefs?

A ☐ Rastafarians will return to their promised land after being slaves in Egypt and Babylon.

B ☐ Rastafarians are one of the twelve tribes of Israel.

C ☐ God came to earth as the black messiah, Ras Tafari.

D ☐ Rastafarians try to live in harmony with nature.

Check your answers.
How many did you get right? ☐ /6

24

How did Rastafarianism begin?
Rastafarianism is a very new religion. It began in 1930 in Jamaica. Marcus Garvey, a Jamaican, predicted there would be a black messiah in Africa. As it turned out Ras Tafari, a prince, became Emperor of Ethiopia in 1930. As emperor he was called Haile Selassie but the name Rastafarianism comes from his name, Ras Tafari. People believed he was the black messiah Marcus Garvey was talking about.

_____

Rastafarians (Rastas) believe in some of the Bible mixed with some African beliefs and traditions. Rastas believe that they are one of the twelve tribes of ancient Israel. They believe that Ethiopia is their promised land. They hope one day to return there just as the Israelites returned to the promised land after being slaves in Egypt and Babylon. Rastas believe that God took human form first as Christ the messiah then as Ras Tafari, the black messiah.

What is the Rastafarian code for behaviour?
Rastas believe in living close to nature. They are vegetarians, and ideally they grow their own food. They do not believe in smoking cigarettes or drinking alcohol or coffee. Interestingly enough, however, they do believe in smoking marijuana or cannabis, since this is to them a natural and beneficial herb. They smoke it as part of their worship.

Where are Rastafarians today?
Most are in Jamaica but Rastafarianism has spread to other Afro-Caribbean communities in Europe and the United States. It especially appeals to young African Americans. The image of the black messiah and the positive message about being black and seeking freedom are very compelling. Although Rastafarians are not a large group, perhaps 100,000, the influence of Rastafarianism has spread beyond its followers through the dress and reggae music of Rastas. Reggae was developed by Rastafarians in Jamaica as an important part of worship. Today you hear it all over the world.

line 1
line 2
line 3
line 4
line 5
line 6
line 7

line 8
line 9
line 10
line 11
line 12
line 13
line 14
line 15

line 16
line 17
line 18
line 19
line 20
line 21

line 22
line 23
line 24
line 25
line 26
line 27
line 28
line 29
line 30
line 31

B Understanding the features of different texts

This section will help you to spot the important features of different types of text so that you can quickly identify texts and understand them. You will learn to:

▷▷ recognise the different features of different types of texts

▷▷ understand how features are used to organise texts

▷▷ work out information from charts and tables.

You will then test your mastery of these skills at the end of the section.

1 How information texts are organised

First read this ...

When you first scan a text:

■ search the text for its features

■ use the features to help you work out what kind of text it is

■ use the features to help you find the information you need in the text.

Now try it!

1 Here are some types of text you will often need to read:

■ memo   ■ advertisement

■ letter   ■ report or essay

■ e-mail   ■ newspaper article

Scan the six texts on pages 17 and 18. Write down what type of text each one is, using the list above. Then note any words or features that helped you work out which type of text it was. The first one has been done for you.

A

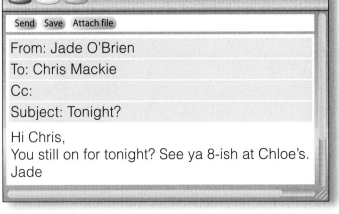

sounds like it's telling you to do something

Experience the new Legato
The pure power of driving passion
Not just a car – a whole way of life.
Leave others standing. Control your destiny!

use of bold text

persuasive words

Text type: ___advertisement___

B

Send   Save   Attach file

From: Jade O'Brien
To: Chris Mackie
Cc:
Subject: Tonight?

Hi Chris,
You still on for tonight? See ya 8-ish at Chloe's.
Jade

Text type: _____

C

SWAPPING A PAPERCLIP FOR A HOUSE!

Just over a year ago Kyle MacDonald thought of a plan to use the internet to see if he could swap things until he ended up with a house …

Kyle, 26, started off by swapping a paperclip for a pen. Then he swapped the pen for a doorknob, and so on. Before long, the whole world was watching to see if he could succeed.

He swapped all kinds of things including an instant party, a camping stove and a holiday. Finally, last week, he made his last swap and got a free house in return for a part in a film!

Text type: _____

D

Date: 1 November 2007

To: Janna Pullman, Maintenance Department

From: David Kearney

Subject: **Cleaning Toilets**

Another client has just complained about the state of the ladies' toilet by reception. This is the third such complaint this week. Please can you do the following?

• Organise a cleaner to clean the toilets at once.

• Find out what the problem is and make sure it doesn't happen again.

Thank you for your help in sorting this out.

David

Text type: _____

E

Mr David Kearney
Manager, Flatmans Ltd
123 Burton Road
Newtown
AG6 4PP

1 November 2007

Dear Mr Kearney

When I visited your company this morning I found the ladies' toilet in a disgusting state. There was rubbish all over the floor, and the sinks were overflowing.

I wish to complain formally about this matter. If you wish to keep my custom, please contact me to discuss this matter.

Yours sincerely

Emily Cameron

Emily Cameron

Text type: _____

F

Insects

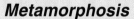

There are more insects than any other type of animal on earth. There are nearly a million species of insect that have been described and given scientific names, and scientists think there are at least seven million more kinds that we do not yet know about.

Insect bodies

The name 'insect' is a good one, because insects have bodies that are **in sect**ions. The three main sections of an insect's body are:

- head
- thorax
- abdomen.

Metamorphosis

Most insects go through a process known as 'complete metamorphosis' as they develop from egg to fully-grown adult. The stages of complete metamorphosis are:

1) eggs
2) larvae (grubs) that look very different from their parents
3) pupae
4) adults.

Text type: _____

2   Read the chart below. It shows some common text features.
    Tick the chart to show which features you found in texts A–F
    on pages 17 and 18. The first column has been done for you.

Feature	Tells readers	Advert	Report	News article	Letter	Memo	E-mail
Main heading	This is the main idea of the whole text.	✔					
Subheading	This is the main point of this part of the text.						
Numbering	You need to understand the points in this order.						
Bullet points	These are different points.						
Paragraphs	The sentences in this part are all about the same idea.						
Bold or italic text	The writer wants you to notice these words.	✔					
Persuasive language	The writer wants you to do something.	✔					
Salutation (e.g. 'Dear Jo', 'Hi, Jo', 'To Jo')	The text is meant to be read by this person.						

3   Read the text below and answer the questions underneath.

Press-ups

A **press-up** or push-up is a common strength training exercise. Press-ups are often used in athletic training, and especially in military physical training.

Different types of press-ups

Full press-ups

This is the standard version of the press-up. It involves:

1 lying face down on the floor
2 placing the hands below the shoulders on the floor
3 keeping the back and legs straight
4 using the arms to raise and lower the body so only the hands and toes are touching the floor.

Easier press-ups

In these versions, some of the body weight is supported so the exercise is easier.

- Wall press-ups are performed by standing close to a wall and pushing away from the wall with the arms.

- Three-quarter press-ups are like a full press-up but with bent legs so the knees touch the ground. These are often used in women's fitness programmes.

Record-breaker

An average male aged 15–19 might be able to do about 25 press-ups without stopping. The world record for non-stop press-ups is 10,508, achieved by Minoru Yoshida of Japan in October 1980.

a) Circle the description that best fits this text:

   newspaper article   report   e-mail   letter   memo   advertisement

b) Why are numbered points used under the heading 'Full press-ups'?

   _____

c) Why are bullet points used under the heading 'Easier press-ups'?

   _____

d) What is the **main** reason why the writer added the subheadings 'Full press-ups' and 'Easier press-ups' below the heading 'Different types of press-ups'?

   A Because the writer wanted to change the subject from 'Different types of press-ups'. ☐

   B Because the writer wanted to make it easier to see what the different types of press-up are. ☐

   C Because the writer wanted to break up the text to make the page look more interesting. ☐

   D Because the writer wanted to show that full press ups are easier than other types of press-ups. ☐

Understanding tables with words and symbols

When you need to find information from a table that uses symbols as well as words:

■ read the heading of each row and column

■ make sure you know what the symbols mean, e.g. by checking the key

■ decide what you need to find out, and find the right row or column to search

■ move your finger along and keep scanning until you find the information.

Now try it!

1 Read the table below, and complete the activities on page 21.

BEACH	BEACH DESCRIPTION	WATER QUALITY	TOILETS (DISABLED)	PHONE	LIFEGUARD	CAR PARK (FREE)	SWIMMING	SEA ANGLING	SUB AQUA	CANOEING	SURFING	CAFÉ	DOG RESTRICTION
St Dogmaels	MF E	NT	WC	☎						✈			
Poppit	S D	E	WC	☎	✂	P	🏃			✈	🏄	✕	🐕
Ceibwr	R S	NT						🐟	🐟	✈			
Newport Sands	S D	E	WC	☎	✂	P	🏃	🐟	🐟	✈		✕	
Newport Parrog	E S R	NT	WC	☎		P		🐟		✈			
Cwm-yr-eglwys	S ST RP	E	WC			P	🏃	🐟	🐟	✈			
Pwll Gwaelod	S SH	G	WC	☎		P	🏃	🐟	🐟	✈			
Lower Fishguard	H	NT	WC	☎		P		🐟	🐟	✈			
Goodwick Sands	S ST	E	WC	☎		P	🏃	🐟		✈			
Aberbach	P S C	NT						🐟					
Abermawr	P S R	E					🏃	🐟			🏄		
Abercastle	R C SH	NT	WC	☎				🐟	🐟	✈			
Aberfelin	SH R C	NT	WC					🐟	🐟				
Porthgain	H	NT	WC	☎		P		🐟	🐟				
Traethllyfn	S R C RP	NT											
Abereiddy	S R C RP	E	WC	☎		P	🏃	🐟	🐟	✈			
Porthmelgen	C R S	NT						🐟					

Key

Beach description:

S Sand beach	**P** Pebble beach	**ST** Stream	**R** Rocky	**RP** Rock pools
E Estuary	**D** Sand dunes	**C** Cliffs	**SH** Shingle	**MF** Mud flats **H** Harbour

Water quality:

E Excellent	**G** Good	**NT** Not tested

a) Can you go surfing at Poppit beach? Yes ☐ No ☐

b) What does this symbol mean? 🐕

_____

c) <u>Underline</u> the name of the beach that has the fewest facilities and activities.

d) Which would be the best beach for a group of people of which some want to swim, some want to surf and some want to go sea angling?

_____

e) Which would be the best beach for a family with children and a dog, who want to go swimming and get drinks and ice creams?

_____

f) Ⓒircle the names of three beaches where the water quality is excellent.

g) What does this symbol 🆆🅲 tell you about the toilet at Goodwick Sands?

_____

_____

h) According to the Beach Description column, what kind of beach is Newport Parrog?

_____

_____

i) Which of the following beaches have streams?

   A Poppit and Ceibwr. ☐

   B Cwm-yr-eglwys and Aberfelin. ☐

   C Cwm-yr-eglwys and Goodwick Sands. ☐

   D Abercastle and Aberfelin. ☐

j) Why did the designer of the table choose to use symbols as well as words?

   A To make the information harder to work out. ☐

   B To make the page look more interesting. ☐

   C So that people who cannot read can understand the chart. ☐

   D In order to fit in more information. ☐

> **Test tip**
>
> When you need to find information in a table, always check carefully so that you know exactly what each row and column is about. Trace along the rows and columns with your finger to find the information you need.

Understanding tables with words and numbers

The way that you find information in a table with numbers is the same as for a table with words and symbols.

■ Read the heading of each row and column.

■ If there are any symbols, make sure you understand what they mean, e.g. by reading the key.

■ Decide what you need to find out. Find the right row or column to search.

■ Move your finger along and keep scanning until you find the information.

▶▶ Now try it!

1 Read the leaflet about the European Athletics Indoor Championships on page 23, and answer the questions below.

Ian wants to book a standard day ticket to see the men's 3000m final. He would like to sit in Area 3 of the arena.

a) On which day does he need to go to the Championships?

_____

b) How much will Ian's ticket cost him?

_____

c) If Ian wanted to see the women's pentathlon, how much would it cost him to buy a ticket to sit in Area 3?

_____

d) How much would it cost to buy a child's ticket to see the men's long jump final, sitting in Area 1 of the arena?

A £20 ☐   B £8 ☐   C £16 ☐   D £15 ☐

e) If Ian wanted to buy a 3-Day pass, which of the following ways would he be able to buy it?

A online ☐   C by phone ☐

B in person from the NEC box office ☐   D by post ☐

f) Which of the following events would you not be able to see if you had purchased a day ticket for the Saturday of the Championships?

A Women's 800m semi-final ☐   C Men's 400m final ☐

B Women's long jump final ☐   D Men's long jump final ☐

Europe's biggest indoor athletics championship is coming to Birmingham. 600 athletes from around 50 countries will compete. The last time the NIA staged a major athletics championship it sold out, so make sure you don't miss your chance!

Ticket Prices

Day Ticket	Gold £	Silver £	Bronze £	Wheelchair £
Friday	20	16	12	16
Concession	-	10	6	10
Saturday	25	20	15	20
Concession	-	15	8	15
Sunday	25	20	15	20
Concession	-	15	8	15

3-Day Pass	Gold £	Silver £	Bronze £	Wheelchair £
Standard	60	48	36	48
Concession	-	34	18	34

Tickets can be purchased by telephone, online or in person from the ICC or NEC box offices.

Please note that all ticket bookings will incur a transaction fee and that 3-Day passes can only be purchased by phone.

Call 0870 739 2007

www.birminghamathletics2007.com

Plan of Arena

 the nia birmingham

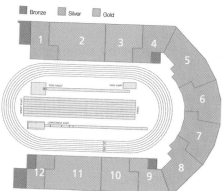

Front cover image courtesy of Mark Shearman.

Daily Highlights Programme

Highlights are included below but please note that this timetable is subject to final confirmation.

Friday
All five events of women's pentathlon
Men's shot final
Men's 60m hurdles final
Women's 60m hurdles final

Saturday
Women's 800m semi-final
Men's 800m semi-final
Women's 60m semi-final
Men's 60m semi-final
Women's high jump final
Men's triple jump final
Men's pole vault final
Women's long jump final
Men's 3000m final
Women's 1500m final
Women's 400m final
Men's 400m final

Sunday
Men's 60m final
Women's 60m final
Final day of men's heptathlon
Women's shot final
Men's high jump final
Men's long jump final
Women's triple jump final
Women's pole vault final
Women's 800m final
Men's 800m final
Women's 3000m final
Men's 1500m final
Women's 4 x 400m final
Men's 4 x 400m final

All information correct at time of print.

Use the test below to find out how well you have mastered the skills in Section B.

To complete this test you will need to use your knowledge of different text features, including charts. You will need to use the text features to help you find the information you need.

These questions are all about the text opposite.

1   Which of the following **best** describes this text?

   A ☐   A newspaper article about diet and exercise.

   B ☐   A report about the advantages of taking exercise.

   C ☐   A persuasive text aimed at persuading people to take exercise.

   D ☐   A report about diets and losing weight.

2   Which of the following would be the **best** heading to use at line 18, as a heading for the chart?

   A ☐   Benefits of exercise

   B ☐   The healthiest types of exercise

   C ☐   Types of exercise and calories they burn up in people of different weights

   D ☐   Calories versus weight

3   What is the **main** purpose of the bullet points at lines 3–7?

   A ☐   They help to persuade the reader.

   B ☐   They make the text look more attractive.

   C ☐   They show that the points follow each other in a particular order.

   D ☐   They make important points stand out clearly.

4   Which of the following statements is **true**, according to the chart?

   A ☐   Skipping burns up more calories than any other exercise in the chart.

   B ☐   Cycling burns up fewer calories than walking.

   C ☐   A person weighing 9 stone would burn up more calories by swimming than by running.

   D ☐   A person weighing 9 stone burns up more calories by running than a person weighing 11.5 stone burns up by cycling.

5   Which of the following statements is **false**, according to the text?

   A ☐   Exercise can help protect people against some illnesses.

   B ☐   Taking exercise can help people who have problems sleeping.

   C ☐   People who weigh less burn up more calories than people who weigh more, when they do the same amount of exercise.

   D ☐   Playing football uses up the same number of calories as cycling.

6 Which of the following text features does **not** appear in this text?

A ☐ Bullet points

B ☐ Main heading

C ☐ Use of italics to emphasise important words

D ☐ Subheadings

◉ For more on text types, headings, numbering, bullet points, and charts and tables, see the Hot Topics CD-ROM.

Check your answers. How many did you get right? ☐ /6

Benefits of exercise

line 1

Regular exercise brings many benefits. Some of the key benefits include:

line 2

- Helping to keep a healthy weight

line 3

- Reducing the risk of serious diseases including heart disease, stroke and diabetes

line 4

line 5

- Improving mood and helping people to feel good

line 6

- Helping people to sleep better.

line 7

Exercise and losing weight

line 8

People who want to lose weight usually have to change their diet. The most efficient way to lose weight is to take in fewer calories through food and drink. However, exercise can also help people to lose weight, and exercising regularly can help people keep to their target weight once they have reached it.

line 9

line 10

line 11

line 12

Exercise and calories

line 13

When people exercise, they burn up calories. To lose weight, a person needs to burn up more calories by exercising than they take on by eating and drinking. Some sorts of exercise burn off more calories than others, as shown by the table below.

line 14

line 15

line 16

line 17

line 18

Activity	Person weighing 9 stone	Person weighing 11.5 stone	Person weighing 14 stone
30 minutes cycling at 12–14 miles per hour	250 calories	307 calories	384 calories
30 minutes walking at 3.5 miles per hour	125 calories	154 calories	192 calories
30 minutes running at 5 miles per hour	250 calories	307 calories	384 calories
30 minutes football	250 calories	307 calories	384 calories
30 minutes swimming	187 calories	230 calories	288 calories
30 minutes skipping	312 calories	384 calories	480 calories

line 19
line 20
line 21
line 22
line 23
line 24
line 25
line 26
line 27
line 28
line 29

C Understanding how writers achieve their purpose

This section will help you to understand more about a range of different types of text, including descriptive texts, explanation texts, persuasive texts and argument texts. It also helps you to focus on:

▷▷ the author's purpose – the reason why they wrote a particular text

▷▷ the audience – the people who will read the text

▷▷ the level of formality of the text – is it formal or informal?

You will then test your understanding of these texts at the end of the section.

1 Identifying audience and purpose

First read this ...

What do we mean by the audience and purpose of a text?

■ **Audience** = **who** it is for, e.g. children, parents, jobseekers, employees ...

■ **Purpose** = **what** it is for, e.g. to inform, to describe, to explain ...

Follow these four steps to identify the audience and purpose of a text.

Step 1	Read the text and decide what it is trying to do (**purpose**). For example, is it: ● describing something? ● explaining something? ● arguing or persuading you to think or do something?
Step 2	Look at the way the text is presented, e.g. headings, pictures, use of bold type. Look out for **text features** that help to tell you what type of text it is.
Step 3	Look for clues that show who the text is aimed at (**audience**). Sometimes it's obvious from the language of the text, and sometimes you will have to search carefully for clues.
Step 4	Look at the **source** of the text – the author, or the book, magazine, leaflet, etc. that it came from. This can often give you clues about the purpose and audience.

▶▶ *Now try it!*

1 Look at the titles below. What kind of text do you think each comes from, and who was it written for? Write the purpose and audience for each one. The first two have been done for you.

a) **How to prevent fires** – by Lincolnshire Fire Service

Purpose: *Explanation about fire prevention*
Audience: *The general public*

b) **Fox Hunting: The Facts – by the League Against Cruel Sports**

Purpose: *Persuasive text to persuade that fox hunting is bad*
Audience: *The general public*

c) **How to choose Primary schools in Buckinghamshire** – from Buckinghamshire County Council

Purpose: _____
Audience: _____

d) *Seduction – the new fragrance by Elements*

Purpose: _____
Audience: _____

e) Why help? - supporting Famine Relief in the Sudan

Purpose: _____
Audience: _____

f) *Fun to Learn with The Banana Gang!*

Purpose: _____
Audience: _____

2 Look at the short pieces of text below. Work out the purpose and audience for each piece of text. The first one has been done for you.

a) For this small maintenance job you will need: a screwdriver, a hammer and a pencil.

Purpose: *To give instructions for a DIY task*
Audience: *People who want to find out how to do DIY*

b) Walk into a room and make your entrance. Revel in the aroma of jasmine, vanilla and a hint of eastern spice.

Purpose: _____
Audience: _____

c) Walking along the dusty road, I can see the colourful saris of the women bustling towards the marketplace.

Purpose: _____
Audience: _____

3 Read this leaflet and answer the questions on page 29.

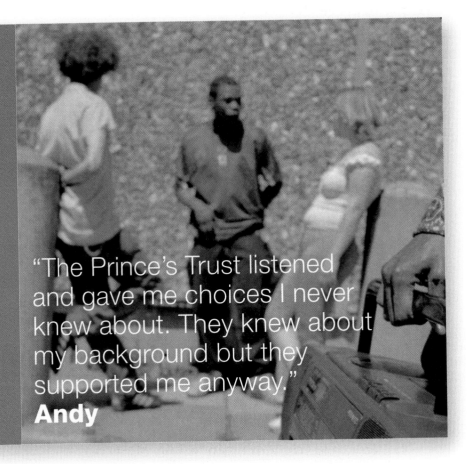

Team-up with The Prince's Trust

Prince's Trust

"The Prince's Trust listened and gave me choices I never knew about. They knew about my background but they supported me anyway."
Andy

What's stopping you from getting on with your life?

Tired, bored or broke?
Not sure what to do?
Don't know where to start?
Then team up with The Prince's Trust

If you are aged 16–25 you could join our Team – a free 12-week programme which will help you move on with your life.

"The Prince's Trust treats you with respect. It's fun. It's a challenge. It gave me so much confidence."
Celina

The Team programme's free to join and you won't lose your benefit.

We offer exciting challenges, which help build your confidence and motivation, give you new skills and qualifications. Taking part will help you get the job you want.

During the programme, you will:
→ Develop practical skills which will help you in life, and in a job
→ Meet new people
→ Enjoy an action-packed week away from home
→ Take part in challenging projects – which you choose
→ Benefit from two weeks' work experience
→ Be given career advice and help with your job search
→ Get help with your CV
→ Make a difference to your local community
→ Achieve nationally recognised qualifications
→ And have an amazing time

Understanding how writers achieve their purpose   c

a) The audience for this text is _____.

b) The source of this text is _____.

The source means the origin of the text – who wrote it, or who was responsible for it.

c) What is the main purpose of this text?

  A To inform young people about the work of The Prince's Trust. ☐

  B To describe the Team programme. ☐

  C To persuade young people to take part in The Prince's Trust Team programme. ☐

  D To present arguments for and against The Prince's Trust. ☐

Test tip

The source is likely to indicate the purpose of the text. Think of the type of document written by charities, the government and other bodies and organisations. Why are they written and for what purpose?

d) (Draw a ring) round a part of the text that gives information on what it costs to join the programme.

e) Which of the following phrases gives factual information about the Team programme?

  A We offer exciting challenges. ☐

  B During the programme, you will … have an amazing time. ☐

  C What's stopping you from getting on with your life? ☐

  D During the programme, you will … achieve nationally recognised qualifications. ☐

f) Which of the following sentences gives an opinion about the Team programme?

  A During the programme, you will … benefit from two weeks' work experience. ☐

  B During the programme you will … have an amazing time. ☐

  C The Team programme's free to join and you won't lose your benefit. ☐

  D Tired, bored or broke? ☐

g) Underline two parts of the text that are persuasive.

h) Which of the following is **not** true, according to the leaflet?

  A The Prince's Trust Team programme is only for people aged 16–25. ☐

  B The Team programme lasts 12 weeks. ☐

  C People who take part in the Team programme have a better chance of getting a good job. ☐

  D People are paid to take part in the Team programme. ☐

First read this ...

Descriptions want readers to picture something. They often:

■ appeal to the five senses – things you can see, hear, touch, taste and smell

■ combine facts and the opinions of the writer

■ contain descriptive language to help the reader picture the topic

■ contain connectives related to time, e.g. *later*, *the next year*, etc.

■ are written in the first person (I) or third person (he/she)

■ contain details of specific times, dates, people and places

■ contain dialogue or quotations from real people.

Now try it!

1 Read this description of a journey in Burma and answer the following questions.

Railway Ties

BY MORRIE ERICKSON

The railway station's platform was teeming with people, choking with cargo. Burmese scrambled in every direction, hands clutching tickets and parcels, like the onslaught of spectators entering a sporting event. Suitcases and tiny children were handed through windows, hands were shaken, families embraced. Porters manhandled bulging rice bags up cramped staircases and through narrow corridors, returning to fetch oversized boxes labeled Sony. Bamboo poles were loaded. So were pottery and woven baskets, crates of oranges, avocados and tomatoes, piles of coiled rope, cages of squawking chickens, bamboo trays of eggs, straw-cushioned cases of Chinese beer, layers of stinking fish. It looked more like an exodus than a journey.

from Salon website

a) Underline three descriptive verbs (like 'teeming') that help you to picture the scene at the railway station.

b) The writer's description of this place and time concentrates mainly on:

A the children in the crowd ☐

B the lively bustling scene ☐

C the smell of the railway station ☐

D the trains ☐

c) The writer's description of the scene makes it sound:

A familiar and everyday ☐

B dangerous and frightening ☐

C exciting and busy ☐

D hot and exhausting ☐

d) Use a wavy line to underline what the writer can smell.

e) Which of the following sentences is a statement of the writer's opinion?

A Bamboo poles were loaded. ☐

B Burmese scrambled in every direction, hands clutching tickets and parcels, like the onslaught of spectators entering a sporting event. ☐

C The railway station's platform was teeming with people, choking with cargo. ☐

D It looked more like an exodus than a journey. ☐

f) Circle a phrase in the text which refers to sounds.

g) Which of the following best describes the tone of the writing in this passage?

A Detached and objective. ☐

B Detailed and descriptive. ☐

C Convincing and persuasive. ☐

D Casual and patronising. ☐

Test tip

Opinions can be thoughts, feelings and attitudes. Opinions can change, and not everyone may agree with them.
Facts describe the way things are or were. Facts generally don't change depending on who is talking or writing about them.

2 Read the descriptive text below. It comes from Letitia Hardy's diary of a year doing voluntary work.

It's <u>January 3rd</u>, my rucksack is packed, strapped up and ready to go. Whatever I have forgotten now, I will have to live without. It is strange that the necessary contents of my life
5 fit in a bag that I will carry with me for the next year. "Passport, tickets, money… passport, tickets, money". I take a deep breath… my mum is waiting downstairs for me, to take me to the airport. A tearful farewell, a few steps and then
10 I am off. I take a final look around my room, haul my bag onto my back and feel a surge of extreme excitement, or is it pure fear?! Either way I feel alive and it is time for the journey to begin.

It is something you memorise by heart, your itinerary,
15 and my first stop was Sri Lanka. This had come about unexpectedly. Having suddenly found myself alone in my quest for travel, I would surf the internet during my clock-watching temp job for stories of inspiration from hot, exotic locations. It was during one of these searches
20 that I stumbled across the website for 'Travellers Worldwide' an organisation that arranges voluntary work abroad.

… Heart pounding, I immediately phoned them for a brochure and more information.
25 They were really friendly on the phone and understood my nerves, and my excitement. I eventually opted for the Sri Lankan placement. It was the appeal of deserted beaches, washing elephants in
30 a river at sunset, ripe fruit, big smiles and a destination so different from England in every way that seduced me. This was the experience I yearned for!

a) Find an example of each of the descriptive features below in the text. Draw a line to link each feature to an example. The first one has been done for you.

- ■ details related to time
- ■ first person
- ■ details of place
- ■ descriptive language
- ■ personal feelings of the writer.

b) Is the phrase 'my rucksack is packed' a fact or an opinion? Tick the correct box.

Fact ☐   Opinion ☐

c) <u>Underline</u> a phrase in this text that you think offers the writer's opinion rather than facts.

d) Which phrase best describes the style of the language in the text?

A Casual and patronising. ☐

B Inappropriate and strict. ☐

C Factual and personal. ☐

D Persuasive and argumentative. ☐

e) This text is used by the travel company Travellers Worldwide on their website. How do you think the text and pictures encourage other young people to do a year of voluntary work?

_____

_____

_____

_____

_____

_____

_____

_____

f) Circle a sentence in the text that is related to the senses (describing things you can see, hear, smell, touch or taste).

g) How did Letitia feel when it was time to start her trip?

A Excited. ☐

B Very sad – she was crying. ☐

C Both excited and frightened. ☐

D Frightened. ☐

h) Why did Letitia decide to go to Sri Lanka?

A She likes eating fruit. ☐

B She wanted to travel to somewhere exotic and very different from Britain. ☐

C She found some information about it on the internet. ☐

D It was the only place she could travel to with Travellers Worldwide. ☐

3 Understanding explanation texts

First read this ...

The aim of an explanation text is to help the reader understand how something is done or why something happens.

A well-written explanation text will often include:

■ precise use of words and sentences and a clear, informative tone

■ technical terms related to the topic

■ connectives that show the order in which things happen, e.g. *first, next, later, then, as a result, finally*

■ headings and subheadings to divide the text up into chunks that are easy to understand

■ tables, diagrams, illustrations and photographs to help the reader see and understand what happens

■ text divided into steps to describe a process, using paragraphs, bullets or numbered points

■ different font styles, sizes and colours to help pick out important words.

Now try it!

1 Answer these questions on the explanation text on page 35.

a) What is the main purpose of this document?

A To persuade people to have tattoos. ☐

B To explain why tattooing is safe. ☐

C To explain the process involved in tattooing. ☐

D To explain how people choose the tattoo they want to have. ☐

b) Who is the main audience for the document?

A Parents who are concerned about their children getting tattoos. ☐

B People who want to choose from a wide range of tattoo designs. ☐

C People who want to find out whether tattoos are safe. ☐

D People who want to understand how the process of tattooing works. ☐

> **Test tip**
>
> Many questions ask about 'documents'. This is a general word for any text you might be given to read.

c) Which sort of illustration would be most helpful to go with this document?

    A A photograph showing different tattoo designs. ☐

    B A table showing the names and phone numbers of local tattoo artists. ☐

    C A diagram showing the process of creating a tattoo. ☐

    D A photograph of a well-designed tattoo. ☐

d) Write a sentence to explain why you think this sort of illustration would be most helpful.

_____

_____

_____

2 Draw lines to show where you can find each of the features listed below. The first one has been done for you.

heading

technical terms

subheading

use of bold text

words that show the order things happen in

process broken up into series of steps

informative tone

How Tattoos Work
By Tracey V Wilson

In this article, we'll look at how the tattoo process works and examine the safety and legal issues surrounding it.

Creating a Tattoo: Outline, Shading and Colour
Clients work with artists to create custom tattoo designs, or they
5 choose images from **flash**, which are tattoo designs displayed in the shop. The artist draws or stencils the design onto the person's skin, since the skin can stretch while the artist uses the tattoo machine. The artist must also know how deeply the needles need to pierce the skin throughout the process. Punctures that are too deep cause excessive
10 pain and bleeding, and ones that are too shallow cause uneven lines.

The tattoo itself involves several steps:

  Outlining, or black work: Using a single-tipped needle and a thin ink, the artist creates a permanent line over the stencil. Most start at the bottom of the right side and work up (left-handed artists generally start on the left side) so they don't
15   smear the stencil when cleaning excess ink from the permanent line.

  Shading: After cleaning the area with soap and water, the artist uses a thicker ink and a variety of needles to create an even, solid line. Improper technique during this step can cause shadowed lines, excessive pain and delayed healing.

  Colour: The artist cleans the tattoo and then overlaps each line of colour to
20   ensure solid, even hues with no 'holidays' – uneven areas where colour has lifted out during healing or where the artist missed a section of skin.

  Final cleaning and bandaging: After using a disposable towel to remove any blood and plasma, the artist covers the tattoo with a sterile bandage. Some bleeding always occurs during tattooing, but most stops within a few minutes.

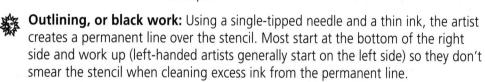

3 Read this text about the law from the Thames Valley Police website for young people. Then answer the questions that follow.

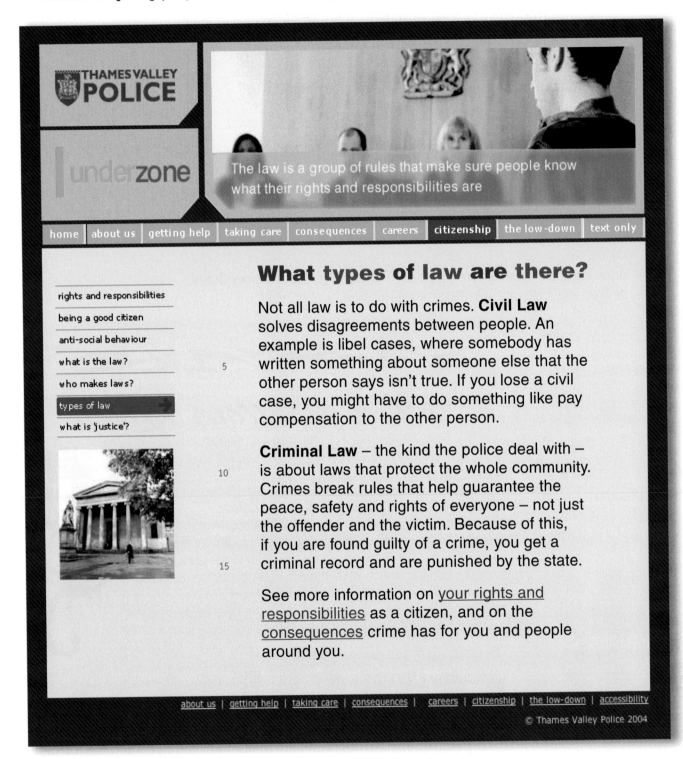

What types of law are there?

Not all law is to do with crimes. **Civil Law** solves disagreements between people. An example is libel cases, where somebody has written something about someone else that the other person says isn't true. If you lose a civil case, you might have to do something like pay compensation to the other person.

5

Criminal Law – the kind the police deal with – is about laws that protect the whole community. Crimes break rules that help guarantee the peace, safety and rights of everyone – not just the offender and the victim. Because of this, if you are found guilty of a crime, you get a criminal record and are punished by the state.

10

15

See more information on your rights and responsibilities as a citizen, and on the consequences crime has for you and people around you.

a) Underline three examples of technical words related to the topic of the text.

b) Use a wavy line to underline a phrase or sentence from the text that gives factual information.

c) Which of the following suggests that this text was written specially for children and young people?

   A The language is clear and simple to understand. ☐

   B The illustrations are jokey and humorous. ☐

   C The text is broken up into small chunks, using bullet points and short paragraphs. ☐

   D The tone of the text is jokey and humorous. ☐

d) Why does this web page use underlined text?

   A To show where the pages link to other information. ☐

   B To make it look eye-catching. ☐

   C To underline important points. ☐

   D To show words that require a dictionary. ☐

e) Which word would best replace the word 'guarantee' at line 11?

   A insure ☐

   B warranty ☐

   C ensure ☐

   D enable ☐

f) Which of the following is not true of libel cases, according to the text?

   A They come under civil law. ☐

   B If you lose one, you might get a criminal record. ☐

   C They involve someone writing something untrue about someone else. ☐

   D They are not dealt with by the police. ☐

g) What is the main topic explained by this text?

   A The consequences if you commit a crime. ☐

   B Your rights and responsibilities. ☐

   C The difference between civil law and criminal law. ☐

   D The kind of law dealt with by the police. ☐

h) Select the phrase that you think best describes the style of the language in the text.

   A Casual and patronising. ☐

   B Inappropriate and strict. ☐

   C Clear and factual. ☐

   D Persuasive and argumentative. ☐

First read this ...

A persuasive text tries to influence the reader to do something or to believe something. Often, a persuasive text will:

- give reasons to make the reader want to do something, e.g. *Be the envy of all your friends!*

- give a lot of opinions and value judgements, e.g. a *brilliant new album – the hottest band since the Arctic Monkeys*

- appeal to readers' feelings, e.g. *Join us today to end this disgraceful situation*

- use imperative verbs that make the text sound as though it is ordering the reader to do something, e.g. *Join today! Explore the city*

- use different types of print to make ideas stand out, e.g. **bold**, colour, CAPITALS, *italics*.

Now try it!

1   Read the following text and draw lines to show where each persuasive feature is. The first one has been done for you.

Facing Closure!

The services that help YOU care for your pets

The Animal Advice Centre runs a wide range of services for pet owners, giving advice on how to care for pets and help with vets' bills in case of hardship. In order to keep the high standards of our services, we depend on the generous donations of our supporters.

5

This year has been particularly difficult for us financially, and now we have a huge challenge. We need to raise £61,000 just to continue providing the services on which so many pets and pet-owners depend.

10

15

For the sake of animals like Blossom, please help us continue with our good work.

Use of colour and capitals for emphasis

Heading to emphasise main message

Words that appeal to the reader's feelings

Request to the reader to do something

Words that express an opinion

Reason why the reader should do something

2   Read the persuasive text below and answer the questions.

Dear Miss Crowe

Union for U!

**GET AWAY THIS SUMMER –
7 NIGHTS FROM JUST £399!**

Welcome to Union Holidays, the UK's number 1 for
unattached single travellers. Discover the world with
new friends when you choose a holiday from one
of the 100+ fabulous destinations featured in our
brochures.

Why not join us on one of the following holidays?
- 17th Jun 2 nights **Rolling Stones** in **Manchester**:
  all ages from £267
- 2nd Jun 7 nights Union holiday **Greece**: all ages
  from £456
- 7th Jun 7 nights Union holiday **Gambia**: 30-59
  years from £789

Book now for a holiday to remember. You won't
regret it!

a)   Underline the phrase in the letter that tells you who
the intended audience for the letter is.

b)   In your own words, say what the letter is trying to
persuade the reader to do.

_____

_____

c)   Circle two examples of imperative verbs that make it
sound as though the text is ordering the reader to do
something.

d)   Which of the following phrases from the letter includes
an opinion?

   A Welcome to Union Holidays. ☐

   B 100+ fabulous destinations. ☐

   C Why not join us on one of the following holidays? ☐

   D Get away this summer. ☐

Come to the funtabulous ...

excitabubbling...

fizziwonderful ...

Amazatorium!

Fed up with dull days out?
Want an action-packed day you'll remember for ever?

Enter the Amazatorium and let your dreams come true!

How will you spend your day? You could

- wander through our tropical rainforest and get up close to the plants and animals

- enjoy the thrill of adventure in our amazing open-air climbing area

- put on a virtual reality headset and enter a wonderful world of your own imagination

- join an underwater guided tour and swim alongside some incredible sea creatures

- experience all the wonder of outer space as you explore the galaxies in our space simulator

- let loose your own creativity as you work with our artists to create an original work of art

With so many options to explore, the incredible Amazatorium offers hands-on fun and excitement for everyone!

a) Who is the most likely audience for this leaflet?

_____

b) What is the purpose of this text?

_____

_____

c) Write down three examples of made-up words in the text.

_____

_____

_____

d) Why do you think the author decided to use these made-up words?

_____

_____

_____

e) Write down two examples of persuasive words (other than the made-up words) that offer value judgements about the Amazatorium to make it sound attractive.

_____

_____

f) <u>Underline</u> an example of a sentence that uses an imperative verb to tell the reader to do something.

g) Which of the following is not a feature of this text?

   A Use of bold and coloured text. ☐

   B Use of persuasive language. ☐

   C Use of word play. ☐

   D Use of numbered points. ☐

h) Which of the following phrases from the leaflet expresses an opinion?

   A work with our artists to create an original work of art ☐

   B How will you spend your day? ☐

   C the incredible Amazatorium offers hands-on fun and excitement for everyone! ☐

   D join an underwater guided tour ☐

i) Which phrase best describes the language of this leaflet?

   A Exciting and persuasive. ☐

   B Factual and informative. ☐

   C Persuasive and formal. ☐

   D Exaggerated and complicated. ☐

First read this ...

Both persuasive texts and argument texts contain **points of view**.

- **Persuasive texts** usually give just one point of view. They aim to persuade the reader to agree with the writer or do what the writer says.

- **Argument texts** usually give more than one point of view on an issue. They present a balanced argument so that the reader can make up his or her own mind. Sometimes the writer states his or her own point of view at the end of an argument text.

Both persuasive texts and argument texts use a mixture of **facts and opinions**.

- **Persuasive texts** usually only include facts and opinions that support the writer's point of view.

- **Argument texts** usually include facts and opinions that support more than one point of view.

Now try it!

1 Read this text and answer the questions that follow.

For many people, visiting a zoo is a good way to have a fun day out while learning about animals. However, other people feel strongly that zoos are cruel and unnatural, and should be closed down.

line 5

Supporters of zoos argue that for animals on the endangered species list, such as pandas and tigers, zoos can be very positive. By keeping these animals in zoos, we can protect them from extinction and learn more about them at the same time. Specialised breeding programmes can be constructed to help increase the numbers of these animals. In time, these endangered animals can be returned to the wild.

line 10

However, opponents of zoos claim that in practice zoos do little to help endangered animals. There are around 4000 different types of animal on the endangered species list, but only around 100 types of endangered animal are being bred in zoos. In reality, very few of these are returned to the wild. It is also claimed that animals raised in zoos are often mentally and physically unfit

line 15

to cope with life in the wild. Opponents of zoos believe that zoo life is at best boring and unnatural for animals; at worst it can actually kill them, make them ill or drive them mad.

a) Is this a persuasive text or an argument text? Tick the correct box.

Persuasive ☐   Argument ☐

b) <u>Underline</u> a sentence that puts across the point of view of opponents of zoos.

c) Ⓒircle the words that best sum up the main point of the second paragraph. (You may need to circle more than one group of words.)

d) Which of the following is **not** a point of view held by supporters of zoos?

A Zoos can be educational. ☐

B Zoos can help endangered animals to breed. ☐

C Zoos protect 4000 different sorts of animals on the endangered species list. ☐

D Zoos can return endangered animals to the wild. ☐

e) Which of the following features can you find in this text? **Tick all that apply**.

A Direct requests to the reader to do something. ☐

B Use of opinions. ☐

C Use of facts. ☐

f) Which phrase best sums up the tone of this text?

A Balanced and even-handed. ☐

B One-sided and biased. ☐

C Strong and confrontational. ☐

D Descriptive and poetic. ☐

g) Here are some phrases from the text.
Put an **A** next to those that express an opinion.
Put a **B** next to those that state a fact.
Put a **C** next to those that use persuasive language.
Put as many different letters next to each phrase as apply.

Zoo life is at best boring and unnatural for animals. _____

There are around 4000 different types of animal on the endangered species list. _____

Zoos can be very positive. _____

Zoos are cruel and unnatural. _____

2　Read this document, which is produced by the Freedom
　　Organisation for the Right to Enjoy Smoking Tobacco
　　(FOREST). Then answer the questions that follow.

Like most people we agree there should be some controls on smoking in public, but a ban
on smoking in most if not all enclosed public places could damage significant sections of the
hospitality industry, including thousands of pubs and restaurants. Despite what the vociferous
anti-smoking lobby would have us believe, such a move is neither popular nor appropriate.

5　According to recent research, 68% of people reject a total ban on smoking in pubs, clubs and
bars (Office for National Statistics) while 71% say proprietors should be allowed to choose
their own policy on smoking (Populus). Options include more no-smoking areas, separate
rooms for smokers, and better ventilation that would allow pubs and restaurants to cater
for smokers and non-smokers alike without affecting business. If you want to fight for choice,

10　visit www.forestonline.org.

FIGHT FOR CHOICE FIGHT THE BAN

To register your support email choice@forestonline.org or visit

www.forestonline.org

6th Floor, 33 Margaret Street, London W1G 0JD

a) Is this an argument text or a persuasive text? Tick the correct box.

Argument ☐　　Persuasive ☐

How do you know?

_____

b) What viewpoint does the document support?

_____

_____

_____

c) <u>Underline</u> the facts that the writer has chosen to support this viewpoint.

d) Which phrase from the text states the writer's opinion?

  A Such a move is neither popular nor appropriate. ☐

  B 68% of people reject a total ban on smoking in pubs, clubs and bars. ☐

  C 71% say proprietors should be allowed to choose their own policy on smoking. ☐

  D To register your support e-mail choice@forestonline.org ☐

e) Which of the following is true according to the text?

  A The writer believes that smoking in public places should not be restricted at all. ☐

  B The writer believes that recent research on people's attitudes to smoking is wrong. ☐

  C The writer believes that restrictions on smoking are neither popular nor appropriate. ☐

  D The writer believes that a ban on smoking in most public places would have bad effects on pubs and restaurants. ☐

f) Which of the following is **not** an option that the writer believes could be used instead of banning smoking in public places?

  A Special areas for people who do not wish to smoke. ☐

  B Separate rooms where those who wish to smoke can do so. ☐

  C Allowing everyone a free choice of whether they smoke and where they smoke. ☐

  D Improving the ventilation in public places. ☐

First read this ...

The choice of formal or informal language for a text depends on audience and purpose.

A **formal** style is usually used for:

- published books
- official letters, e.g. to or from companies
- speaking or writing to (including e-mailing) people you don't know personally, particularly if they are important.

An **informal** style is usually used for:

- people you know well
- e-mailing friends and acquaintances
- texting.

Some texts are written in a style that combines formal and informal, e.g. persuasive or information texts for young people.

Now try it!

1   Look at the text features in the list below. Put **F** by each feature that you would expect to find in a formal text. Put **I** by each feature that you would expect to find in an informal text.

Slang	_____	Easy short words	_____
Complex sentences	_____	Short, simple sentences	_____
No contractions (e.g. *do not*, not *don't*)	_____	Passive verbs (e.g. *The shoplifter <u>was</u> <u>requested</u> to leave the shop*)	_____
Incomplete sentences	_____	Contractions (e.g. *don't, won't*)	_____
Technical terms	_____	Abbreviations (shortened words e.g. *thru*)	_____

2   Look at this list of texts. Put **F** by each text you would expect to be written in a formal way. Put **I** by each text you would expect to be written in an informal way.

Slang	_____	An e-mail inviting a friend to a party	_____
A job application by e-mail	_____	An e-mail inviting a friend of your grandmother's to a party	_____
A job application by letter	_____		
A text to your sister	_____	A letter to the local newspaper	_____
A memo giving important business information	_____	A magazine article about fashion for teenagers	_____

3 Read the sentences below. Underline the formal words with <u>straight lines</u> and the informal words with w̰a̰v̰y̰ ̰l̰ḭn̰ḛs̰. You only need to underline one or two words in each example. The first two have been done for you.

a) We're taking the k̰ḭd̰s̰ to the park.

b) He <u>divulged</u> the <u>scenario</u> eventually.

c) He was eyeing up the talent in the pub.

d) The date with him was wicked.

e) You're sad if you like reggae.

f) I would be grateful if you could send me more details. Yours faithfully, Jane.

g) I am writing to confirm my resignation.

h) He's really starting to bug me.

i) I'm sick of it all! I quit!

j) The saline solution was added to the liquid in the test tube.

k) Please acknowledge receipt of this letter.

4 Now read this e-mail, which Helen Martin sent to the Marsden Hotel to book her hen night. The tone is too informal. Circle any areas where she has used inappropriate language.

Write a more formal version of this e-mail in the space below.

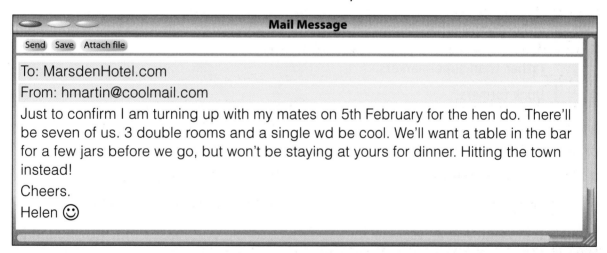

Mail Message

Send Save Attach file

To: MarsdenHotel.com
From: hmartin@coolmail.com
Just to confirm I am turning up with my mates on 5th February for the hen do. There'll be seven of us. 3 double rooms and a single wd be cool. We'll want a table in the bar for a few jars before we go, but won't be staying at yours for dinner. Hitting the town instead!
Cheers.
Helen ☺

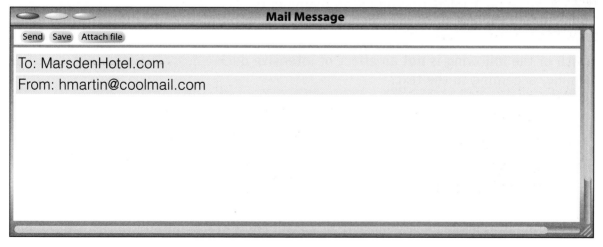

Mail Message

Send Save Attach file

To: MarsdenHotel.com
From: hmartin@coolmail.com

Use the test below to find out how well you have mastered the skills in Section C.

To complete this test you will need to use your knowledge of different text types. You will also need to focus on the author's purpose in writing the text, the audience intended for the text and whether it is formal or informal.

⊙ For more on the features of different text types, see the Hot Topics CD-ROM.

These questions are all about the text opposite.

1   What is the main purpose of this document?

A ☐ To persuade the reader not to eat duck.

B ☐ To explain about the different types of feeds given to ducks.

C ☐ To explain why it is best to buy ducks at a butcher's.

D ☐ To persuade the reader not to buy intensively farmed ducks.

2   Who is likely to be the main audience for this document?

A ☐ Meat-eaters who are concerned about animal welfare.

B ☐ Committed vegetarians.

C ☐ People who want to support local businesses rather than supermarkets.

D ☐ Duck farmers.

3   Which of the following best sums up the main point of the paragraph that starts at line 10?

A ☐ Soya-based feeds should be avoided.

B ☐ The duck's diet affects the flavour of its meat.

C ☐ Free-range ducks have the best flavour.

D ☐ Some duck feeds contain cheap ingredients like fishmeal.

4   Which of the following is **not** an effect of intensive duck-farming, according to the text?

A ☐ Poor flavour and texture of duck meat.

B ☐ Ducks that dream of swimming on a pond.

C ☐ Reduced quality of life for ducks.

D ☐ Use of cheap feeds instead of more expensive, healthier feeds.

Ducks

Compared to chickens, the market for farmed ducks may seem small but, at twenty million birds reared per year in the UK, it is still quite large enough to have encouraged the development of highly intensive production units. Needless to say, they have driven the birds' quality of life, and in turn the eating quality of their meat, to a pitifully low standard. Most ducks can't even dream about swimming on a pond, because they'll never get to see one in their short and sorry lives.

More even than chicken, the taste and texture of duck reflect the quality of the bird's diet. The use of cheap, soya-based feeds tends to produce flabby and insipid meat, while feeds bulked with fishmeal (as many are) will pass on a distinctly unsavoury fishiness to the flesh. In contrast, a bird fed on a good grain-based diet, with access to natural forage, will shine through in terms of flavour.

People tend to buy a duck 'for a change', in the expectation that it will be a bit of a treat. There is really no point in buying one unless it is going to fulfil this promise. So, as a minimum, you are looking for a free-range bird that has been grain fed until nice and plump, creating a layer of fat that keeps the meat beneath succulent and helps the skin above roast to a fabulous crispness. You are more likely to find a bird like this at a good butcher's than a supermarket.

(line 1 – line 24)

5   What was the author's purpose in writing the sentence that starts on line 7?

A ☐ To make the reader feel sorry for intensively farmed ducks.

B ☐ To put the reader off eating duck.

C ☐ To compare the lives of intensively farmed ducks with the lives of free-range ducks.

D ☐ To make duck farmers feel guilty.

6   Which words best sum up the tone of this document?

A ☐ Balanced and factual.

B ☐ Chatty and informal.

C ☐ Persuasive and informative.

D ☐ Technical and argumentative.

Check your answers.
How many did you get right? ☐ /6

40

D Spelling words correctly

This section will help develop your spelling skills by:

⮞⮞ giving you rules for the correct spelling of words

⮞⮞ giving you strategies for remembering spellings

⮞⮞ giving you practice in spelling words correctly

⮞⮞ helping you spot when words are wrongly spelt.

You will then test your knowledge of these skills at the end of the section.

1 Spelling strategies

❚❚ First read this ...

You can use lots of different methods for remembering the correct spelling of words. Different methods suit different words and different people. Read the suggestions on page 51.

⮞⮞ Now try it!

Read this draft explanation of spyware. Look carefully at the 12 words in bold. Some of them are spelt correctly, some incorrectly. Write each word in the relevant column in the table below. Use the spelling strategies on page 51 to help you.

Spyware

Spyware is **softwear** that gathers information about a user, **usually** without their **knowlidge** or informed consent, and then passes this data to others.

As with **computer virises**, spyware comes in various forms, but much of what is commonly **referred** to as spyware is **currantly** perfectly legal.

The information it gathers is used by **busnesses** to target users with tailored **avertising**, interrupt their online experience with **annoying** pop-up windows and bombard them with unwanted **emales promoting** products and services.

Words spelt correctly	Words spelt incorrectly – write the correct spelling!

Learn to spell words as you meet them
This is the best method of all!
Use the 'Look – Say – Cover – Write – Check' method.

Use a memory aid
*nec*ess*ary* – 1 *c*ollar and 2 *s*leeves
*ac*comm*o*dation – *c*osy cottages and *m*agnificent *m*ansions
*sep*a*rate* – there is *a rat* in sep*a*rate

Group words in their families
e.g. same letter patterns:
light, *bright*, *night*, *sight*, etc.
or other versions of the same word:
definite, finite, definitely

Break the word up into syllables
(good for long words)
ad-ver-tise-ment
un-u-su-al
re-le-vant

Spot links between similar words
here, *where*, *there* (all refer to place)
*tri*cycle, *tri*angle, *tri*pod (all refer to three)

Over-emphasise
Pronounce the tricky or silent letters when you say the word to yourself.
(good for silent letters)
Wednesday
February
government
recognise

Remember tricky pairs of words together
insure (pay money in case of accident), *ensure* (make sure), e.g. *Ensure you insure your iPod.*

computer (-er), *monitor* (-or), e.g. *Is it a computer – er – or is it a monitor?*

believe (-ie), *receive* (-ei), e.g. *I believe I will receive a free plastic gnome.*

accept (take), *except* (apart from), e.g. *We accept all forms of payment except credit cards.*

currant (dried grape), *current* (all other meanings), e.g. *The current situation is that all the currants have been eaten.*

List ten words that you find difficult to spell, and practise spelling them!

1	6
2	7
3	8
4	9
5	10

Plurals

First read this ...

Plural means *more than one* of something. To make a word into a plural you usually add 's':

■ iPod → iPods

■ mobile phone →mobile phones.

However, there are lots of exceptions. The activities below will help you to deal with these exceptions.

Now try it!

1 Read the table below carefully. Complete the examples in the third column.

Words that end with ...	Spelling rule/hint	Examples
-s, -x, -z, -sh, -ch	Add -es *Hint:* These words end with a hissing, shushing or buzzing sound. The plurals add another syllable to the word.	bus → buses bush → bushes A fox → _____ B bench → _____ C wish → _____ D fizz → _____
-y	For words ending in a *consonant* + y, change -y to -ies. For words ending in a *vowel* + y, add -s.	army → armies volley → volleys E party → _____ F accessory → _____ G diary → _____ H gameboy → _____
-f, -ff, -fe	Change -ff to -ffs. Change the others to -fs or -ves. *Hint:* Say the plural aloud. A 'v' sound means the word should end -ves.	leaf → leaves riff → riffs reef → reefs I belief → _____ J cliff → _____ K thief → _____
-o, -oo	Some words ending in -o add -s, some add -es. Words ending in -oo always add -s. *Hint:* You need to learn which -o words are in each group!	potato → potatoes patio → patios disco → discos kangaroo → kangaroos L tomato → _____ M tattoo → _____ N radio → _____

Test tip

Don't forget – some words remain the same in the plural, e.g. *sheep, fish, deer.*

2 Some words change completely in the plural. (Circle) the correct spelling in each case.

A He's got two left foot/foots/feet.

B The women/wimen/wimmin were separated from the mans/men/mens.

C She came home with one chicken and two goose/gooses/geese.

D Who is going to look after the childs/childers/children?

3 Some of the book titles below have been spelt incorrectly. Cross out the incorrect book titles and write the correct spellings underneath the misspelt titles.

Brief lifes of the great inventors

———————————————

Coaches, 1850–1950

———————————————

The master chefs of southern France

———————————————

Flies and fly-fishing

———————————————

Kangaroos and Wallabies

———————————————

Thiefs and Swindlers

———————————————

Factorys in the Midlands

———————————————

How to bake loaves and cakes

———————————————

Ladys and Gentlemen: how to make an after-dinner speech

———————————————

Nightmare Scenarioes — brushs with death in the jungle

———————————————

Human Dynamoes

———————————————

Words that sound the same

Many common words sound the same but have different meanings and are spelt differently. You need to learn the spellings of these words.

Now try it!

1   There, their and they're

   ■ **There** means *in*, *at* or *to* a place, or goes with the verb *to be* to show that something *exists*.

   ■ **Their** means *belonging to someone* or *belonging to a group of people*.

   ■ **They're** is a shortened form of *they are*.

   Fill in the blanks with the correct word.

   A Would you like to put the shopping bags over t_____?

   B Don't worry. T_____ parents will be here to pick them up soon.

   C I think that t_____ a lovely couple.

   D T_____ are boy bands better than that.

   E I'm sure that t_____ coming.

   F I think that I can hear t_____ car pulling up outside.

2   To, too and two

   ■ **To** means *towards* or *in order to*.

   ■ **Too** means *as well* or *excessively*, e.g. *It's all too much!*

   ■ **Two** is the *number 2*.

   Circle the correct spelling in each case.

   A If you're too/to/two nervous, you won't perform your best.

   B Jake wanted to go too/to/two both gigs.

   C Too/To/Two's company, but three's a crowd.

   D Use the bridge too/to/two cross the rail track.

   E Her intention was too/to/two break the school record.

3 Are and our

■ **Are** is part of the verb *to be*.

■ **Our** means *belonging to us*.

Add the correct words in the spaces provided.

> We _____ going on holiday with _____ friends tomorrow.
> _____ bus leaves at 10 a.m. and we _____ pretty certain
> we'll get to _____ hotel by _____ planned time of 8 p.m.
> _____ you sure that you don't want to join _____ party?

4 Who's and whose

■ **Who's** is short for *who is*.

■ **Whose** means *belonging to whom*.

Write one sentence using 'who's' and one sentence using 'whose'. Make sure you spell them correctly!

A _____

_____

B _____

_____

5 Wear, where, were and we're

■ **Wear** is to *be clothed* in, as in *I'm wearing jeans*, or to *weaken*, as in *everyday use will wear it out*.

■ **Where** means *in which place*.

■ **Were** is the past tense of *are*.

■ **We're** is short for *we are*.

The writer of the text below has confused all her wear/where/were/we're spellings. Write the correct spelling in the bracket in each case.

> I know you we're (_____) going to come shopping
> with me, but I've gone on my own. I don't want to go
> were (_____) we usually go, and I don't want you
> telling me what to where (_____). To be honest I
> don't know wear (_____) our relationship is going:
> wear (_____) not seeing eye to eye at the moment,
> are we? It we'res (_____) me out just thinking
> about it.

4 Suffixes and double letters

A *suffix* is a group of letters that can be added to the end of a word to form another word. For example, -ing, -er, and -ed are all suffixes, e.g. *dancing*, *dancer*, *danced*.

Follow these rules when you add suffixes to words.

1 a) If the last syllable of the word is stressed (emphasised when you say it out loud), has a single vowel and ends with a consonant ...
      ... then double the last letter before the suffix.

   ■ forbid → forbidden, forbidding ←——————— *Letter d is doubled here*

   b) If the word has only one syllable, has a single vowel, and ends with a consonant...
      ... then double the last letter before the suffix.

   ■ stop → stopped, stopping ←——————— *Letter p is doubled here*

   Add the suffixes -ing and -ed to the word 'flag':

   _____

2 If the last syllable of the word is not stressed ...
   ... then do not double the last letter.

   ■ benefit → benefited, benefiting ←——————— *In 'benefit', the first syllable is stressed, not the last syllable – so t is not doubled.*

   ■ gallop → galloped, galloping

   Add the suffixes -ing and -ed to the word 'gossip':

   _____

3 If the last syllable of the word has two vowels ...
   ... then do not double the last letter.

   ■ repeat → repeated, repeating ←——————— *Two vowels in the last syllable so letter t is not doubled.*

   ■ gloat → gloated, gloating

   Add the suffixes -ing and -ed to the word 'bead':

   _____

4 If the word ends with an -e ...
   ... then omit the -e when you add -ed, -ing, -ation or -able:

   ■ fake → faked, faking

   ■ recite → reciting, recitation

   ■ excite → excitable

   Add the suffixes -ed, -ing and -ation to the word 'inspire':

   _____

Now try it!

5   The writer of this draft advert has made some spelling mistakes. Look at all the underlined words and tick the ones that are correct. Cross out the ones that have been spelt wrongly. Write these misspelt words correctly underneath.

Imagine ...

Imagine <u>waking</u> up in your apartment, on a marina in the south of France. There are palm trees all around, and boats are <u>carveing</u> their way through the water. Imagine <u>strolling</u> to the <u>mooreings</u> only metres away where the boats are waiting to take you for a morning's water-<u>sking</u> or, <u>possibley</u>, <u>diving</u> in delightfully warm water. Imagine a safari around the magnificent gulf, <u>visiting</u> Saint Tropez, Port Grimaud and Saint Maxime, or <u>anchoring</u> off a beautiful cove to snorkel and swim in the azure sea, or <u>sunbatheing</u> in the <u>scorching</u> sun. Imagine mountain <u>bikeing</u> across open vineyards and along forest tracks. Visit the most beautiful Provençal villages in France, where the views across the gulf to the Alpes Maritime beyond are <u>stuning</u> and the ride back down <u>exhilarateing</u>! Imagine evenings <u>sitting</u> on your terrace, <u>siping</u> a glass of irresistible French wine, <u>watching</u> the sun <u>seting</u> behind the local Maures mountains…Perfect.

Write the misspelt words correctly here:

_____

_____

_____

_____

Use the test below to find out how well you have mastered the skills in Section D.

To complete this test you will need to use your spelling skills. You will need to remember the spelling rules and strategies that you have learnt for remembering correct spelling.

The draft article on the opposite page needs to be proof read because there are eight spelling errors. Read the draft article and answer the questions that follow.

1 Which is the correct spelling of **unfortunatly** in line 3?

   A ☐ unfortunatlie

   B ☐ unfortunitely

   C ☐ unfortunately

   D ☐ unfortunatelly

2 Which word would best fill the gap on line 3?

   A ☐ there

   B ☐ their

   C ☐ ther

   D ☐ they're

3 Which spelling would best fill the gap in line 7?

   A ☐ aloud

   B ☐ allowed

   C ☐ alloud

   D ☐ alowed

4 What is the correct spelling of **weather** on line 16?

   A ☐ wether

   B ☐ wheather

   C ☐ wever

   D ☐ whether

5 What is the correct spelling of **entill** on line 19?

   A ☐ untill

   B ☐ until

   C ☐ entil

   D ☐ antill

Employing school aged children

line 1

Millions of children who are at school at the moment have part-time jobs.
Unfortunatly, many of them don't know that _____ breaking the law.

line 2
line 3

For example, did you know that children are not allowed to have a job if they are under 12 years old? Also, children are not _____ to work during school hours.

line 4
line 5
line 6
line 7

There are laws to protect children at work:

line 8

- They must not work before 7 a.m. or after 7 p.m. on a school day.

line 9
line 10

- They must not work for more than two hours on a Sunday.

line 11
line 12

- They must not lift heavy objects in case of injuries.

line 13
line 14

But children are being put at risk because they don't know **weather** or not they are breaking the law. For example, 10% of school-aged children with jobs have skived school in order to work. Many children work **entill** after 7 p.m. on school days. Children and the owners of the _____ they work for may **sincerley** believe there is no problem. But this is an important issue which _____ everyone in the workplace.

line 15
line 16
line 17
line 18
line 19
line 20
line 21
line 22
line 23

6 Which spelling would best fill the gap on line 20?

A ☐ busnesses

B ☐ businesses

C ☐ busynesses

D ☐ bissinesses

7 What is the correct spelling of **sincerley** on line 21?

A ☐ sincerly

B ☐ sincerley

C ☐ sincerely

D ☐ sinserley

8 Which spelling would best fill the gap on line 23?

A ☐ effects

B ☐ efects

C ☐ affects

D ☐ afects

Check your answers.
How many did you get right? ☐ /8

48

E Using punctuation correctly

This section will help you to improve the punctuation in your own writing. It will also help you to spot and correct punctuation mistakes in the test. You will learn how to:

- write complete sentences
- use full stops, exclamation marks and question marks
- use commas, apostrophes and inverted commas
- write in paragraphs.

You will then test your mastery of these skills at the end of the section.

1 Sentences

First read this ...

When you are writing, using correct sentences helps your reader understand your ideas. In the test you will need to be able to correct any sentences that are not right.

There are four basic types of sentence. All begin with a capital letter. Note the punctuation marks at the end:

- **Statements**, e.g. *The CD costs £14.99.* ← _____ full stop at the end
- **Questions**, e.g. *How much does this CD cost?* ← _____ question mark at the end
- **Exclamations**, e.g. *It's only £14.99!* ← _____ exclamation mark at the end
- **Commands**, e.g. *It's only £14.99 – buy now!* ← _____ exclamation mark may be used

To be complete, a sentence needs to make sense on its own and include a verb.

For example, this is a sentence: 'My dad's into jazz.' ← _____ The verb is 'is', shortened to 's, and the words make sense.

This isn't a sentence: 'For some reason.' ← _____ There is no verb, and the words don't make complete sense on their own.

For more on sentences and making sense, see Section F1.

▶▶ Now try it!

1   Read the sentences below and add the right punctuation and capital letters to each. The first one has been done for you.

a)   We crept up very quietly and made her jump.

b)   how many times have i asked you not to do that

c)   you should have seen him blush

d)   go to your room at once

e)   it all began one dark and stormy night

2   Read this draft document and answer the questions that follow.

> We are a well-established local company. With over 40 years'
> experience of painting and decorating. You can rely on Stokes, whether
> you want a completely new look for your whole house, or a makeover
> for just one room? No job is too small or too large for our dedicated
> 5 team of professional decorators. We offer a full interior design service,
> with advice on all the latest styles. Don't let your house get stuck in the
> past. Are you thinking of updating your style. Do you want to be the
> envy of your neighbours? Or sell your house quickly? Then call Stokes
> today. We are waiting for your call, with over 100 satisfied customers
> 10 locally, we are the decorators most people rely on. You have nothing to
> lose and everything to gain. Why not ask us for a quote today?

a)   What is the problem with the words 'With over 40 years'
     experience of painting and decorating.' on line 1?

   A They make a very short sentence. ☐

   B They should end with an exclamation mark. ☐

   C They should end with a question mark. ☐

   D They are not a complete sentence. ☐

b)   On which line has a question mark been wrongly used?

   A line 4 ☐   B line 6 ☐   C line 7 ☐   D line 10 ☐

c)   On which line has a comma been used where a full stop
     should have been used?

   A line 3 ☐   B line 5 ☐   C line 8 ☐   D line 9 ☐

d)   Which line contains an incomplete sentence?

   A line 4 ☐   B line 6 ☐   C line 8 ☐   D line 10 ☐

e)   Which line has a sentence that should end in a question
     mark?

   A line 1 ☐   B line 3 ☐   C line 5 ☐   D line 7 ☐

f)   The writer of this draft document has not used any
     exclamation marks. Find two sentences that could end with
     exclamation marks, and write these in.

2 Commas

First read this ...

You need to know when to use commas, and you need to be able to spot when commas have been missed out or wrongly used in a text.

a comma separates each item

- A comma is used to separate items in a list, e.g.
  The sports shop sold clothing, footwear, rucksacks, equipment and books.

  'and' is used instead of a comma to link the last two items in the list

- Commas are used to separate out extra information that has been added into a sentence, e.g.
  Fahim and Hasan, the owners of the shop, are selling their business.

  commas separate out the additional information

  to check whether the commas here are used correctly, say the sentence without the information inside the commas. It should still make a sentence on its own: Fahim and Hasan are selling their business.

- A comma is used to separate clauses (a clause is a main part of a sentence; each clause has a verb):
  Although Keith was fit, he couldn't reach the summit.

  this is one clause (note the verb 'was')   *this is another clause (note the verb 'couldn't')*

Now try it!

1 Read the gym information leaflet below.

   a) Mark the job each comma in paragraph 1 is doing by putting the appropriate letter in each box:

   A – a comma used to separate items in a list

   B – a comma used to separate out extra information added into the sentence

   C – a comma used to separate clauses.

   b) Add five commas to the text in paragraph 2 so that it makes sense.

We all need time to relax and look after ourselves, whether it's a break from the kids, work or the general routine. Come to the Ranleigh Health and Fitness Centre, just behind Tesco's, and we will provide some peace, tranquillity and space for you to enrich your lifestyle. Ranleigh Health Club is for adults only, so all areas of the club are guaranteed as peaceful and relaxing.

Ranleigh Health Club offers an extensive range of fitness equipment: treadmills rowing machines weights machines and free weights. The gym area overlooks the tennis courts so you can watch the games while you get yourself fit. The pool 25 metres long is accompanied by a sauna and spa area.

2 Read this draft extract from a parenting advice booklet and answer the questions.

To smack or not to smack?

It is important that children learn how to control their own behaviour as they get older, [A] parents are important role models for their children in helping them to learn how to do this.

Every parent experiences frustration with his or her child at various times, a parent will often feel tempted to smack in the heat of the moment. But this is an outlet for the parent's frustration rather than a helpful way of influencing the child's behaviour.

However, [B] simply because lots of people may have smacked their children this does not mean it is the best way to punish your child or ensure good behaviour. Those who say smacking is unacceptable, [C] often argue that it is more helpful and safer to notice and reward your child's good behaviour, to encourage the behaviour you want.

Needless to say, in this society parents are not allowed to physically harm their children. Parents who continue to smack their children, may simply not know about other methods that work.

a) Look at [A]. The word 'parents' is the subject of a new sentence, so a comma should not be used before it. **Replace the comma with a full stop and add a capital letter for 'Parents', to make a new sentence.**

See Section F3 for more help with subjects and verbs

b) **Find another example** in the next paragraph where this mistake has been made. **Correct the punctuation there** in the same way.

c) Look at [B]. Notice the correct use of a comma after this word. Similar words or phrases that begin sentences are 'Of course', 'In addition', 'On the following day', etc. **Find and circle another example of this use of the comma in the final paragraph.**

d) Look at [C]. 'Those who say smacking is unacceptable' is the subject of the sentence. Never put a comma between the subject of a sentence and the verb ('often argue'). Where has this mistake been made again in the final paragraph? <u>Underline</u> **the comma that is used wrongly in this way.**

3 Apostrophes – the basics

▌▌ *First read this ...*

An apostrophe looks like this: '

There are two rules for using the apostrophe.

1. **Omission.** The apostrophe is used to show that a letter is missing when two words have been made into one word. Sometimes an apostrophe shows that two or more letters are missing.

   I am → I'm

   can not → can't

2. **Possession.** The apostrophe is used to show that something belongs to someone or something. Add 's after the word that shows who the owner is.

   <u>*The player*'s *shirt*</u>

   <u>*The player*'s *hand*</u>

   <u>*The player*'s *position*</u>

   When the owner is in the plural and ends in -s, add an apostrophe after the -s.

   <u>*The players*'</u> *celebration* ⟵ *there are lots of players*

I can't believe we won the match! I'm so happy!

▶▶ *Now try it!*

1   One apostrophe of omission has been underlined and connected to its original word pair. <u>Underline</u> any other examples of apostrophes for omission and connect them to their original word pairs by drawing a line.

How is

It is —

I have

I have

Mail Message
Send   Save   Attach file
From: emilymatik@brimail.co.uk
To: amyessen@brimail.co.uk
Subject: Hi!
Hi Amy! <u>It's</u> ages since we spoke. Just checking that everything's all right with you all. I've just bought a new computer that I'm pretty excited about. I was getting sick of fighting for time on **Trisha's** machine. How's James's new job going? I was hoping to visit sometime soon to see you all. I'll try to remember to bring the twins' CD that they left here last time. I wouldn't want you to think I've pinched it!
Hope to see you soon,
Emily

I am

would not

I will

everything is

2

Read the café blackboard and answer these questions.

a) Cheryls café should be written:

A Cheryls' café ☐

B Cheryl's café ☐

C Chery'ls café ☐

D Cheryls café' ☐

b) Todays £4 specials should be written:

A Today's £4 specials ☐

B Todays £4 specials ☐

C Todays' £4 special's ☐

D Todays £4 special's ☐

c) Fish and chip's with mushy pea's should be written:

A Fish and chip's with mushy peas ☐

B Fish and chips with mushy peas ☐

C Fish and chips' with mushy peas' ☐

D Fish and chips with mushy pea's ☐

d) Dont delay – come in today! should be written:

A Do'nt delay – come in today! ☐

B Dont delay – come in today! ☐

C Do n't delay – come in today! ☐

D Don't delay – come in today! ☐

e) You're fish is our command! should be written:

A Youre fish is our command! ☐

B You'r fish is our command! ☐

C Your fish is our command! ☐

D You're fish is our command! ☐

Test tip

Remember: there is no apostrophe in plural words, even if they end in a vowel.

pianos not **piano's**

paninis not **panini's**

bananas not **banana's**

First read this ...

1

Q For apostrophes of possession, do you still add 's' to a noun if it already ends in s?

A When a noun ends in 's' you can either add ' or 's, e.g. **Chris'** CD or **Chris's** CD.

2

Q If a plural doesn't end in 's', where do you put the apostrophe of possession?

A Just add **'s** to the word, e.g. the **men's** department, **children's** clothes.

3

Q What is the difference between **its** and **it's**?

A Remember – the apostrophe in **it's** is for omission: it's stands for 'it is', e.g. it's a breeze! **Its** (no apostrophe) is used to show possession, e.g. **Its** enormous scaly tentacles ...

Test tip

- **Its** is the **exception to the rule** about using an apostrophe for possession. It often causes confusion. **Remember: There is no apostrophe when something belongs to 'it'!**
- When in doubt, read the sentence replacing **its/it's** with **it is**. If it sounds right, you need to use **it's**, e.g. The dog lost it's bone is wrong because it doesn't make sense to say The dog lost it is bone. **Just remember that it's = it is** and you won't go wrong.

Now try it!

1 Where have apostrophes been used incorrectly or missed out in these notices? Write out the word correctly under each notice.

ITS THE LAW
PLEASE LEASH, CURB
AND CLEAN UP
AFTER YOUR DOG!

_____

_____

GENTLEMENS' CLOAKROOM

_____

JAMES ROOM

_____

2   Read through the website below, which provides information about an under 18s club night in Cambridge. Nine of the words have been underlined: put a tick or a cross in the box to show if the punctuation is correct. If it is incorrect, write out the correct spelling.

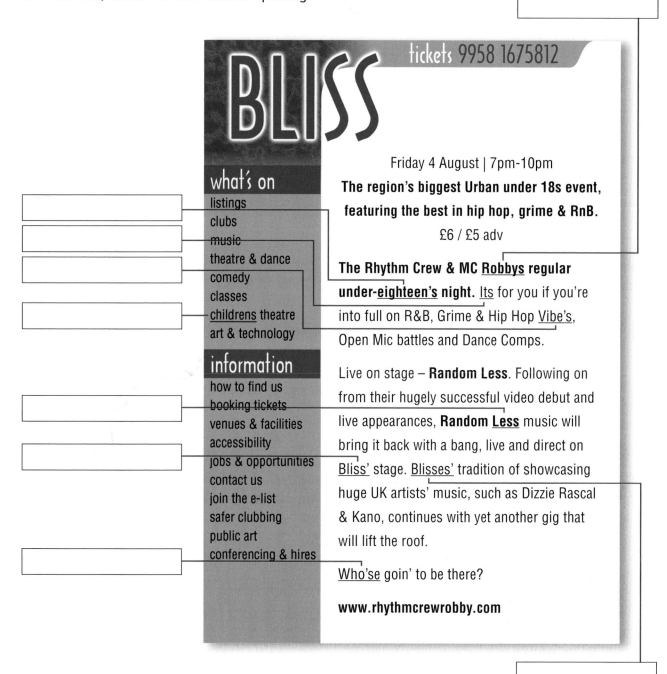

3   Read this passage. Look carefully at each 'its', and add apostrophes where necessary.

> Its a cold night and the moon is out, its shape clear through the trees. The old house stands empty and silent. Part of its roof is lying on the ground and part is hanging off as though its about to fall at any moment. Its a weird old place. Its rafters are sound, its brickwork is secure, yet its creepy.

5 Inverted commas

First read this ...

Inverted commas are used to show the reader three things:

1. That words inside inverted commas are a quotation of the words someone said or wrote, or a piece of text quoted from somewhere else, e.g. *The notice in the shop window said '50% off everything today'. 'Wow!' she said, in amazement.*

2. That the words are the title of a book, newspaper, play or film, e.g. *I was reading 'The Dungeon of Trelawney'.*

3. That this word or phrase is slang, or used in a special way, e.g. *He thinks he's a 'dude'.*

> **Test tip**
>
> • Sometimes you will see two inverted commas used together ("Wow!") and sometimes just one ('Wow!'). Both are right.
> • Inverted commas are sometimes called 'speech marks' or 'quote marks'.

Now try it!

1 Look at the film review below. The examples of inverted commas are underlined. Write a number (1, 2 or 3) in the text boxes to link each example to one of the three uses of inverted commas mentioned above. The first one has been done for you.

'Donnie Darko' [2]

For his debut feature, writer-director Richard Kelly certainly didn't lack ambition. It's a 'teen' movie combined with science fiction and thriller elements. It's a twisted combination of 'American Beauty' and 'Fight Club'. When this strange bunny creature that haunts the film informs him that the apocalypse is less than a month away, and a jet engine mysteriously falls on his house, a warped tale begins. Despite all the darkness, the story is lifted by a 'down-to-earth' romance with a new girl (Jena Malone) in school. The director makes the character's torment all too real, but that's not to say that Donnie's a big 'mope'; he's remarkably smart, and his dark wit is razor sharp.

'Creepy, funny, poignant, and stunningly imaginative', says Bart Lemovich of 'Film Monthly', and I have to agree. Rent it!

Inverted commas are often used for quotes in novels and newspaper reports. This is also called 'direct speech'. The inverted commas are only used when the *actual words spoken* are quoted.

2 Read this extract from the draft of a novel and answer the questions.

> Just as Kofi opened his mouth
> to speak, the car sped away.
>   Nadine ran up, puffing and
> panting. 'We'll never catch
> 5 them now!' she gasped.
>   Kofi muttered that if only
> Nadine had got a move
> on, this would never have
> happened.
> 10   So, what do we do now? Nadine asked.
>   Kofi started to say that they'd better get the bus home,
> but Nadine said that he was being boring.
>   Well, you think of something, then, Kofi grunted.
>   Nadine told him that 'she'd had about enough of him
> 15 expecting her to come up with answers to everything.'
>   Just then, Kofi remembered something very important.

a) On lines 4–5, 'We'll never catch them now!' are the actual words spoken. How do you know?

_____

_____

b) The exact words that Kofi said are not given in lines 6–9, so inverted commas are not used. What would his exact words have been?

_____

_____

c) Where should the inverted commas be on line 10? Mark them in the correct places.

d) Is there any direct speech on lines 11–12?

Yes ☐   No ☐

e) Add the inverted commas correctly on line 13 to show the direct speech.

f) Why is it a mistake to use inverted commas on lines 14–15?

_____

_____

Test Tip

Put inverted commas around words that were actually said. Don't forget – you need inverted commas at <u>both</u> ends of the words. Remember to start speech with a capital letter and end with a question mark, full stop or comma. Make sure you put full stops, exclamation marks etc. inside the inverted commas. "Speech marks hold it all together!"

First read this ...

A paragraph is a group of sentences about one main idea. Paragraphs are a way of organising a longer text on one subject into smaller sections. Start a new paragraph for:

■ a new topic

■ a new place

■ a new time

■ a new speaker.

Now try it!

1   Read through this welcome letter to a new member of Marsden Gym and answer the questions on page 71.

Mr Brendan Licher
7 The Close
Leeds
LE5 4EL

MARSDEN GYM

1 November 2007

Dear Brendan

May I take this opportunity to give you a warm welcome to Marsden Gym. I am sure you will enjoy our excellent facilities and be well supported here in improving your health and fitness.   paragraph 1

I can confirm that your membership started on 30 October and will be due for renewal on 30 October 2008. I will write to you nearer the time. Please note that the joining fee only needs to be paid once, so you will only be paying the subscription fees from now on.   paragraph 2

I hope you have had a chance to sample the excellent range of healthy snacks in our café. Many of our members find this a great way to set themselves up with a routine of good exercise and healthy eating. I note that you have not yet booked an induction session with your personal trainer, Alan. Do please take advantage of this high-quality service we offer all our customers. Alan has extensive experience of fitness and body building and will be very pleased to support you in developing a personal programme. I hope that you enjoy your membership with us. If you have any queries, please do not hesitate to contact me.   paragraph 3

Yours sincerely

Carol

Carol Winchester

a) Why has the writer started a new paragraph at paragraph 2?

_____

_____

b) The third paragraph is too long. Mark with // where you would break it into three separate paragraphs.

2   This draft text about the explorer Ranulph Fiennes needs to be broken up into five paragraphs.

a) Mark with // where each paragraph should begin.

Sir Ranulph Fiennes

Sir Ranulph Fiennes was born on March 7th 1944, shortly after his father was killed in action during World War II. After the war his mother moved the family to South Africa, where Ranulph lived until he was 12. After school in Britain he served eight years in the
5   British army, followed by service in the private army of the Sultan of Oman. Ranulph has been an explorer and adventurer since the 1960s. He led hovercraft expeditions up the White Nile in 1969, but he completed his most famous trek in 1979–1982, when he and Charles Burton travelled round the world, from pole to pole, using
10   only surface transport. They covered 52,000 miles and became the first people to have visited both poles. Ranulph then joined up with a nutrition specialist called Mike Stroud. In 1993 they took 97 days to cross Antarctica unaided. This is the longest journey in south polar history. In 2000 Ranulph tried to walk on his own to the North Pole.
15   However, his sleds fell through the ice and he had to pull them out by hand. This led to severe frostbite in his fingertips, and he had to abandon the expedition. Back at home, Ranulph cut off his dying fingertips with an electric saw in his garden shed. Four months after a heart operation in 2003, Ranulph bounced back to run seven
20   marathons in seven days, one on each continent of the world. The first race, on 26th October, was in South America; the final race, on 1st November, was in North America. The most difficult race was in Singapore, Asia. Ranulph's expeditions have raised a great deal of money for good causes. He was awarded the OBE in 1993 'for
25   human endeavour and for charitable services'.

b) Write the number of each paragraph next to the subtitle below that you think best describes that paragraph.

On his own	_Number_
Early life	_Number_
Charitable endeavour	_Number_
Explorer and adventurer	_Number_
Marathon man	_Number_

Use the test below to find out how well you have mastered the skills in Section E.

For more on using paragraphs, see the Hot Topics CD-ROM.

To complete this test you will need to use your knowledge of punctuation, including how to use full stops, exclamation marks, question marks, commas, apostrophes and inverted commas. You will also need to know how to compose complete sentences and write in paragraphs.

These questions are all about the text opposite.

Read through the draft letter opposite and then answer the following questions.

1   What correction should the writer make on line 1?

   A ☐ Change the full stop after 'complaints leaflet' to a comma.

   B ☐ Change the 'And' to 'and'.

   C ☐ Take out the full stop and change 'And' to 'and'.

   D ☐ Change 'complaints' to 'complaint's'.

2   The punctuation mark missing on line 3 is:

   A ☐ a comma after 'TV'

   B ☐ a full stop after 'yesterday'

   C ☐ a comma after 'yesterday'

   D ☐ inverted commas around 'DVD'

3   The commas on line 10 are to:

   A ☐ mark off the words from the rest of the sentence

   B ☐ show where the reader needs to take a breath

   C ☐ make a list of relevant items

   D ☐ separate two clauses in the sentence

4   There are errors in apostrophe use on lines:

   A ☐ 1, 3 and 9

   B ☐ 3, 6 and 7

   C ☐ 3, 5 and 9

   D ☐ 6, 7 and 9

Dear Sir/Madam

I have read through your customer complaints leaflet. And understand that you | line 1
need a formal letter outlining the reasons for my dissatisfaction. | line 2

I ordered two item's which arrived yesterday The TV and DVD player are | line 3
hopeless. The TV, is only giving a picture on one side of the screen and | line 4
the DVD player, started getting very hot after being on for only 20 minutes. | line 5
It then melted my sons The Best of Paddington DVD. I followed all the | line 6
instructions in the accompanying booklets, so theres no way this is my fault. I | line 7
would be grateful if you would send someone to collect the equipment as soon | line 8
as possible. I am available on Mondays, Wednesdays and Fridays. Can you | line 9
confirm, at your earliest convenience, that someone will come on one of | line 10
those days. | line 11

Yours sincerely | line 12

Leanda Robertson | line 13

5 Which line should contain a pair of inverted commas?

A ☐ line 1

B ☐ line 6

C ☐ line 7

D ☐ line 3

6 A new paragraph should begin at:

A ☐ line 1

B ☐ line 4

C ☐ line 5

D ☐ line 7

7 On which lines have commas been used in error?

A ☐ lines 7 and 9

B ☐ lines 1 and 3

C ☐ lines 10 and 11

D ☐ lines 4 and 5

8 On which line should a question mark be added?

A ☐ line 2

B ☐ line 7

C ☐ line 9

D ☐ line 11

Check your answers.
How many did you get right? ☐ /8

F Using good grammar

This section will help you to use good grammar in your writing. It will also help you to spot when a sentence does not make sense, or is unclear. You will learn:

▷▷ how to use connectives (joining words)

▷▷ how to choose the right tense for your verbs

▷▷ how to make sure that the subject and verb agree

▷▷ how to use pronouns clearly.

You will then test your mastery of these skills at the end of the section. See Section E1 for more help on writing proper sentences.

1 Using connectives

❚❚ First read this ...

Connectives are joining words that can be used to link sentences, or to link different parts within a sentence. Words like 'and', 'but', 'although', 'because' and 'when' are all connectives.

Using the right connectives can help make your sentences much clearer. Instead of simply using 'and', try a word such as 'although', 'because' or 'when'. For example:

■ She hurried and they had already gone. ✗

■ She hurried, but they had already gone. ✔

■ Although she hurried, they had already gone. ✔

'and' just connects two ideas – it doesn't tell you anything about how they are connected

'but' and 'although' suggest there is a problem or a down-side

▷▷ Now try it!

1   Add the appropriate connecting word from the box, so that these sentences make good sense.

   A She snacked too much after school, _____ she's not hungry now.

   B _____ he arrived late, the manager gave him a verbal warning.

   C _____ you left, I read until midnight.

   D Kieran studied very hard, _____ get a good degree.

   E He went out for a walk, _____ it was still raining.

> **after:** tells you the order in which things happen
>
> **although:** shows that something happens even though there is a problem
>
> **because:** shows the reason something happens
>
> **so:** shows what happens as a result of something else
>
> **in order to:** shows the reason why something is done

2   Rewrite these pairs of sentences as one sentence. Write in the right connective from the box. The first one has been done for you.

a) She frightens me. She is so outspoken.

She frightens me because she is so outspoken.

b) We'll need to leave at six. We can be sure we'll get there on time.

_____

c) He'll need to save £5 a week. He wants to buy the bike himself.

_____

d) He sent a pass down the touchline. Beckham was there to intercept it.

_____

3   Read the text below, and then answer the questions.

> What is a celebrity? Some people would say celebrities are people who are famous for doing nothing, but is this fair? Although some celebrities, such as many actors, musicians and sportspeople, are genuinely talented, there are many others who don't seem to do anything except appear on reality TV shows.
> line 5   Why do we care about these people? It seems we have a love-hate relationship with celebrities. We can't seem to stop watching them! Many people say they only buy the magazines and watch the shows in order to laugh, but secretly they really enjoy keeping tabs on what their favourite celebrities are doing.
>
> _____ the high visibility of celebrities' personal lives, their failures are often
> line 10   made public. Perhaps this is the down-side of modern celebrity – the price they pay _____ they can continue in the public eye.

a) Find four connectives in the first paragraph, and underline them.

b) Which connective could best be used after 'celebrities' on line 6, to join the two sentences?

A because   ☐   B after   ☐

C and   ☐   D in order that   ☐

c) Which connective could best be used to fill the gap on line 9?

A Although   ☐   B Because of   ☐

C After   ☐   D So that   ☐

d) Which connective could best be used to fill the gap on line 11?

A after   ☐   B until   ☐

C so   ☐   D because   ☐

First read this ...

The tense of a verb tells us **when** an action happens. It can be in the past, present or future.

Past	Present	Future
Yesterday I **walked** to work.	Today I **am taking** the bus.	Tomorrow I **shall get** a lift.

When you choose what tense a verb should be in, you need to think about whether the sentence is referring to the past, present or future. When you are talking about the same event or group of events in your writing, make sure that you stick to a single tense – past, present or future.

Now try it!

1   Read the draft school magazine report below. It explains how a peer anti-bullying group was set up in Drayfield Manor School. Circle the correct option in each case to ensure that all tenses are written correctly.

Remember to think about whether the sentence is talking about something that *has* happened, *is* happening now or *will be* happening.

> At Drayfield Manor School a peer anti-bullying group was set up last year to support pupils who **were/are/will be** experiencing bullying. In
> 5 January the Year 12 tutor **asked/asks/will ask** for six volunteers to lead the group. They then **worked/work/will work** with representatives from each year group to look at the results of a bullying survey that had been sent to all pupils.
>
> Last March the representatives **were/are/will**
> 10 **be** given training on how to support other pupils who are experiencing bullying. This training **was/is/will be** highly successful. A qualified counsellor from the organisation 'Stamp out Bullying' **taught/teaches/will teach** our pupils
> 15 about how to support their peers.
>
> Now anyone from Year 7–11 who **was/is/will be** experiencing bullying **found/can find/will find** the pupil counsellors each day at lunchtime and after school.

Think: what difference does 'Now' make?

2   Read the letter Marie has written to a magazine problem
    page and answer the questions below.

Star Letter

Doc – I'm 12 yrs old and with three other girls I bully another girl. We
still all hang around together. The girl that we bully is our friend but
we are all nasty to her. We all try to be nice to her, but we just can't.
We pick on her and say nasty things to her.

In the beginning she was more like one of the group and we all have a good   line 5
time together. We spent break and lunch time together and at the weekends we
go shopping.

Now, even though we still spend time together, we just can't help being
unpleasant to her. Last week we even tried to get rid of her by falling out with
her – we <u>tell</u> her to find new friends and then she <u>goes</u> off crying. Will she ever   line 10
forgive us?

a)   On lines 1–4 is Marie referring to:

   A   the past

   B   the present

   C   the future

   D   a mixture

b)   On lines 5–7 Marie is inconsistent in her use of tense.
     Which tense should she stick to?

   A   The past

   B   The present

   C   The future

   D   A mixture

c)   On lines 5–7, which two verbs are in the wrong tense?

   A   have and go

   B   was and have

   C   was and spent

   D   spent and go

d)   On line 10 the two underlined verbs are in the wrong
     tense. They should be:

   A   are telling and is going

   B   will tell and will go

   C   told and went

   D   tells and went

First read this ...

Remember that the subject and the verb of every sentence must agree. This means that you have to use the right form of the verb to suit the subject. For example, this is the verb 'to score', in the present tense:

I score   we score
you score   you score
he/she/it scores   they score

So if you want to write about one footballer scoring a goal, you write:

He scores. ✔

'He' is the subject so 'scores' is the verb

not   He score. ✘

You also need to make sure that singular nouns go with singular verbs, and plural nouns go with plural verbs. For example:

It is a brilliant goal. ✔

There is only one goal so you need to use 'is', which is a singular verb.

It are a brilliant goal. ✘

Now try it!

1   Read the draft text of a job advert. There are six errors in subject-verb agreement. Underline the errors and then write the correct words above each one.

Fitter for Excellent Bodyshop
based in central London

Our firm is an established London Bodyshop. We are seeking an experienced Fitter who work locally and can move between our two garages in North London. You has a minimum of 3–4 years experience within a Bodyshop and must have your own tools. You is a good communicator, self-motivated and able to meet targets and deadlines.

You will work in a friendly team with other Fitters, and the job are replacing damaged bodywork and stripping and fitting door panels, wheel arches, bumpers and trims. If you is looking for a fantastic opportunity to progress in a fast expanding company and has the experience and skills required, contact us now.

E-mail motor@bradbury.co.uk

---

2 Here are some things to look out for in subject-verb agreement. Put ticks against the correct sentences, and crosses against the incorrect sentences, in each case.

a) Some common verbs are irregular – e.g. _I have_ becomes _he has_, not _he haves_.

- ■ They goes to the cinema every Thursday. ☐
- ■ Katherine does make an effort to phone regularly. ☐

b) 'Nobody', 'every', 'everybody', 'either … or' all take singular verbs, e.g. _Everybody_ **is** _here_.

- ■ Either my brother or my cousin are going to the match with you. ☐
- ■ Nobody really wants to stay that late. ☐

c) Two singular nouns added together take a plural verb, e.g. _Ant and Dec seem to be everywhere._

- ■ Federer and Roddick are the best tennis players on the circuit. ☐
- ■ Hannah and two of her friends has gone away for the weekend. ☐

c) The verb must agree with the noun that is the subject of the sentence. You may have to read the sentence carefully to work out which noun is the subject, e.g. _Waiting times for a patient in A&E are often as long as two hours._

The subject is 'waiting times' (plural) not 'patient' (singular), so it's right to use a plural verb ('are').

- ■ Teachers' skills in developing their pupils' creativity varies from school to school. ☐
- ■ The attendance level in all our courses has risen hugely. ☐

3 All these sentences are in the present tense. Add the right verbs. Make sure the verbs and subjects agree!

a) Abdul and Karim _____ going to the match.

b) Every packet of crisps _____ been eaten.

c) Everybody _____ going clubbing.

d) My complaint about the deliveries _____ being ignored.

4 Using pronouns clearly

First read this ...

Pronouns allow you to refer to a noun without repeating that noun, e.g. *Raj turned to Greg and asked **him** a question*, rather than *Raj turned to Greg and asked **Greg** a question*.

There are many different pronouns. Look at the box on the right.

It is important to keep pronouns consistent in your writing so that your reader knows which nouns they refer back to.

> First person pronouns =
>   **I, we, my, our**
> Second person pronouns =
>   **you, your**
> Third person pronouns =
>   **he, she, it, they, him, his, her, its, their**

Now try it!

1   Put a tick or a cross after each sentence. Circle the noun that the pronouns refer to. Make sure that the correct pronoun has been used – it has to match the noun that it refers to. The first one has been done for you.

  a) The course teaches (young adults) how *you* should care for *your* babies. ✗

  The course teaches (young adults) how *they* should care for *their* babies. ✓

  b) You should put the baby to bed before *he* gets tired. ☐

  You should put the baby to bed before *they* get tired. ☐

  c) Students should bring an example from *their* own experience. ☐

  Students should bring an example from *your* own experience. ☐

  d) As soon as Dave opened the door, *you* could see that there had been a break-in. ☐

  As soon as Dave opened the door, *he* could see that there had been a break-in. ☐

  e) Mina asked Neelam and Navid if *they* could help her. ☐

  Mina asked Neelam and Navid if *she* could help her. ☐

2   Read these sentences and circle the nouns that can be replaced by a pronoun. Write the correct pronoun after each sentence.

  a) Gina could hardly believe how many people turned to look at Gina. _____

  b) The tree was creaking loudly, as if the tree was about to fall down. _____

  c) Chloe and Sam went to the party where Chloe and Sam had a great time. _____

3　Read these draft 'frequently asked questions' to go on a website about karting.

The main noun in each case is marked in red. Check that the pronouns referring to the nouns are correct.

Circle any incorrect pronouns and add any corrections in the margin.

The first one has been done for you.

Check out below to see if we've answered your question already. If they are not here, then contact us.

'Question' is singular, so it needs a singular pronoun. 'They' is a plural pronoun. It should say 'it is'.

How big is the circuit?

　It is over 1 mile long.

Is there anywhere spectators can watch from?

　Our circuit has a seated paddock area for spectators. They offer great views of the track.

What time do I need to arrive for booked events?

　Participants must arrive 20 minutes before the event. Otherwise we might not be allowed to participate.

What karts do you use?

　We use 200cc biz karts for organised events. We also have 120cc JB Junior karts for 8–13 year olds. This is the safest for this age.

How fast do the karts go?

　We go at over 40 mph. Fast enough when you're sitting in them!

What happens to the event if it rains?

　It is not cancelled. It goes ahead rain or shine!

Can women race?

　Of course she can!

Test your skills

Use the test below to find out how well you have mastered the skills in Section F.

To complete the test you will need to use your knowledge of how good grammar can improve your writing. You will also need to use connectives correctly, choose the right tense for your verbs, make subject and verb agree and use pronouns properly.

These questions are all about the text opposite.

1   On which lines have pronouns been used wrongly?

A ☐   lines 6, 9, 12 and 22

B ☐   lines 3, 6, 17 and 22

C ☐   lines 3, 9, 18 and 21

D ☐   lines 6, 19, 21 and 22

2   Which connective could best be used to join the two sentences on lines 3–4?

A ☐   although

B ☐   so

C ☐   but

D ☐   because

3   Read lines 12–15 carefully. Which verb is not written in the correct tense?

A ☐   painted

B ☐   decorated

C ☐   begins

D ☐   given

4   The word 'works' on line 17 should read:

A ☐   worked

B ☐   working

C ☐   work

D ☐   are working

5   Which word should be used in place of 'her' on line 22?

A ☐   his

B ☐   their

C ☐   our

D ☐   theirs

Nail technician information sheet

The work

Being a nail technician can be a rewarding and creative job. There is plenty of opportunity to use both design skills and people skills in a friendly atmosphere.

Nail technicians apply false nails and nail extensions, and decorate it using different techniques.

The customer's nails are first checked for signs of skin or nail disease. If it shows signs of either, extensions or false nails cannot be applied. The technician then discusses with the customer the most suitable type of nail extension and any decoration required.

Then work begins. First the nails are cleaned to ensure it is free from bacteria. Then the client are given a manicure. Finally, the technician decorated the nails in different ways, e.g. applying gems, colours, glitter or designs painted freehand or with an airbrush.

Hours and environment

Nail technicians works around 37 hours a week. This often includes weekend work.

Nail technicians sometimes work alone. They can also work in a salon with other technicians, or beauticians. Some nail technicians are self-employed, either working from home or visiting clients in her own homes.

There are no minimum qualifications to be a nail technician. Salons are likely to require NVQ/SVQ qualifications.

What to do next

Several local courses will begin for new trainees this September. Interested applicants is interviewed in July. If you want to find out more, please phone for an information pack.

line 1
line 2
line 3
line 4
line 5
line 6
line 7
line 8
line 9
line 10
line 11
line 12
line 13
line 14
line 15
line 16
line 17
line 18
line 19
line 20
line 21
line 22
line 23
line 24
line 25
line 26
line 27
line 28

6   Which connective could best be used to join the two sentences on lines 23–24?

A ☐ because
B ☐ so
C ☐ until
D ☐ although

7   The word 'is' on line 27 should read:

A ☐ are being
B ☐ will be
C ☐ were
D ☐ have been

Check your answers.
How many did you get right? ☐ /7

64

G Preparing for the test

This section will help you get ready to take the test. It will help you make good use of all the skills you have practised in the other sections of the book. You will find out:

▶▶ how to work out what a question is asking you to do

▶▶ how to tackle different types of questions

▶▶ how to identify and answer questions about spelling, vocabulary, grammar and punctuation.

1 How to work out what a question is asking you to do

First read this ...

Before you sit the test you should:
- be familiar with the style of the questions you will answer in the test
- identify exactly what a question is asking you to do.

Now try it!

A Remind yourself of the multiple-choice question style. Read the text on page 85 and the question below, and look at the labels. Then find and tick the correct answer.

> This tells you about the text you are going to read. It is important to know what kind of text it is in order to be able to answer these questions.

Test tip

The Council's 'main aim' is their intention, so the right answer is the one that best describes their intention. Some of the other answers may *result from* this intention – but these things are not the main aim.

Questions 1–10 are about this extract from a Council leaflet on a green waste recycling scheme.

1 What is the Council's main aim in setting up this scheme, according to lines 1–12?

A ☐ To reduce the amount of waste going into landfill sites.

B ☐ To make it easier for people to recycle.

C ☐ To make compost.

D ☐ To avoid contributing to global warming.

> Each question has four possible answers. Only one of them is right but the other three may appear to be right if you don't read them carefully enough. Make sure you check all four answers before deciding which is right, and don't just guess – try to work it out!

Three good reasons to sign up for the Council's new green waste recycling scheme

line 1
line 2
line 3

1 We have decided to provide this scheme in order to make recycling easier and more convenient for you.

line 4
line 5

2 By joining the scheme you can help ensure that less green waste ends up in landfill sites across the District. In landfill sites, green waste breaks down to form leachate, a harmful liquid that can pollute water and soil, and methane, a greenhouse gas that contributes towards global warming.

line 6
line 7
line 8
line 9
line 10

3 At the moment, you may find it both time-consuming and difficult to take your green waste to the tip. If you sign up for the scheme, your green waste will be collected from you, and you can be sure that it will be put to good use to make compost which will benefit the environment.

line 11
line 12
line 13
line 14
line 15

We can collect most types of green waste, but there are some definite no-nos. Please see the back page for more details.

line 16
line 17

How will the scheme work?

line 18

The scheme will run from April 2007 to March 2008. Waste will be collected once a fortnight from outside your property on a designated weekday for your area. On registration, you will be provided with a calendar that clearly shows which weeks and collection day your bin will be emptied. Once collected, your green waste will be taken to a commercial composting facility where it will be turned into compost. The compost produced does not belong to the Council and the Council does not make a profit from its sale.

line 19
line 20
line 21
line 22
line 23
line 24
line 25
line 26
line 27
line 28

The questions may ask you to look at specific lines so each line of the text is numbered to help you find your way around it.

B Multiple-choice questions can be written in several different ways, and you need to know how to answer each type. Read the descriptions below and then answer Questions 2 and 3 on page 86.

■ The question may be written as a question, ending in a question mark. Suggested answers A–D then simply show possible answers to that question. An example of this is Question 1 on page 84.

■ The question may be written as the beginning of a sentence that needs to be completed. You must choose the correct ending to complete the sentence. All the answers will make sense but only one answer completes the sentence correctly. An example of this is Question 2 on page 86.

■ The question may ask you to identify something that is **not** true according to the text. Questions of this sort often use words like 'Which of the following is not …'. An example of this is Question 3 on page 86.

2 The main problem with putting green waste in landfill sites is that:

A ☐ it is time-consuming and inconvenient

B ☐ it results in by-products that can harm the environment

C ☐ it means you can't make compost from the green waste

D ☐ not all types of green waste can be collected

3 Which of the following is <u>not</u> an intended outcome of the green waste scheme?

A ☐ Making compost.

B ☐ Making people's lives easier.

C ☐ Improving the environment.

D ☐ Making money for the council.

Test tip

Be particularly careful of questions like Question 3 that ask you what is **not** true. Decide on what you think the correct answers are so that you can recognise the incorrect answer in the options given to you. You need to be very careful to read all the options before deciding which is the odd one out.

C In the test you will often find questions that focus on the **purpose** of a text – to explain, describe, persuade, etc. Questions 4 and 5 show two different ways that questions about purpose can be written.

4 The statement that best describes the purpose of the recycling leaflet on page 85 is:

A ☐ to inform and persuade

B ☐ to inform and explain

C ☐ to describe and argue

D ☐ to advise and argue

5 Which of the following best describes the author's intention in writing this leaflet?

A ☐ To persuade local people to use the scheme.

B ☐ To argue that recycling will benefit the local area.

C ☐ To inform local people about how the scheme works.

D ☐ To argue that the local area is highly polluted.

Test tip

- Often, the text will have more than one purpose, e.g. to explain and persuade, or to inform and entertain. You then need to consider which pair of purposes given in the suggested answers is the best fit for the text.
- Questions about purpose sometimes use the words 'author's intention'.

D Test questions can also focus on the **audience** for a particular text – the people for whom it was mainly written, e.g. children, parents, teenagers, the general public, men at risk of heart disease. Questions focusing on audience may use phrases such as 'written for', 'intended for', 'likely readers', etc., as well as 'audience'. Question 6 is an example of a question focusing on audience.

> **6** The main audience for the recycling leaflet is:
>
> A ☐ local residents
> B ☐ people who don't have time to take their waste to the tip
> C ☐ people who care about the environment
> D ☐ businesses in the local area.

Test tip

Some of the suggested answers may be very similar, but only one is correct. Don't tick the first answer you think might be right. Read through all the choices and match them carefully against the text before you make your decision. Remember you are being asked for the **main** audience.

E Test questions often focus on the **language** and **tone** of a text. Questions may ask you to pick the best description of the tone of the text (objective or subjective, humorous, poetic, balanced or biased, etc.). Questions may also focus on the type of language used, e.g. formal or informal.

Look out for these words that are often used to describe the tone of a text.

■ **Objective:** factual and unemotional – the writer is stating the facts and presenting a balanced argument.

■ **Impersonal:** similar to objective – the writer does not reveal a particular viewpoint or address the reader as 'you'.

■ **Subjective:** a personal tone, where the author is clearly writing from one viewpoint and not presenting a balanced argument.

■ **Biased:** similar to subjective, where the author presents a one-sided viewpoint.

■ **Argumentative:** the writer presents one viewpoint forcefully and contradicts other viewpoints.

■ **Analytical:** the writer weighs up all the facts and considers the information carefully.

■ **Sensational:** the writer overstates things and uses exaggerated language.

■ **Colloquial:** the writer uses very informal language, similar to spoken language.

■ **Patronising:** the writer assumes that the reader is ignorant or childish and 'talks down' to them.

■ **Academic:** the writer presents a balanced viewpoint using formal and technical language.

■ **Clear:** the writer explains carefully and gives examples that are easy to understand.

Questions 7–9 are examples of questions focusing on language and tone.

> **7** The tone of the green waste scheme leaflet is mostly:
>
> A ☐ factual and impersonal
> B ☐ subjective and biased
> C ☐ analytical and informative
> D ☐ factual and informative.

8 The language of the green waste scheme leaflet is mostly:

- A ☐ formal and clear
- B ☐ informal and chatty
- C ☐ colloquial and personal
- D ☐ formal and academic

9 Which of the following phrases from the document is informal in tone?

- A ☐ Designated weekday.
- B ☐ Commercial composting facility.
- C ☐ Definite no-nos.
- D ☐ You can be sure.

F Some questions ask you to say what the appropriate response to a document would be. Generally, these questions want you to choose a form of response that is at the same level of formality as the document itself. Question 10 gives an example of this.

10 What is the most appropriate way to respond to the green waste scheme leaflet?

- A ☐ A business letter.
- B ☐ A personal letter.
- C ☐ A memo.
- D ☐ Filling in a form.

Test tip

Usually the right kind of response will match the original document. For example, if it is a leaflet, you might fill in a form; if it is a business letter or personal letter then you might write the same sort of letter back.

Questions 11–14 are about this explanation on the subject of composting, found on a local council website. Read the text and then answer the questions below, which focus on the organisation of the text.

How does composting work?

line 1
line 2 Composting is a natural process that turns
line 3 organic material (things that were once living)
line 4 into rich soil-like material called compost.
line 5   The organic material is broken down by
line 6 microorganisms such as bacteria, fungi, insects
line 7 and worms and by chemical reactions. The
line 8 process generates heat as decomposition takes
line 9 place, and the more heat that's generated, the
line 10 faster decomposition occurs!
line 11   To work properly, composting needs lots of
line 12 air and moisture. The composting process is
line 13 known as 'aerobic decomposition', which means
line 14 decomposition in the presence of air. (If this
line 15 happens without the presence of air, it is known
line 16 as anaerobic decomposition. It's this type of rotting that produces bad smells
line 17 and a slimy, smelly mess rather than good compost.)
line 18   There needs to be a good balance of carbon and nitrogen for the material
line 19 to be composted well. Too much of either one will result in poor compost.

The composting process

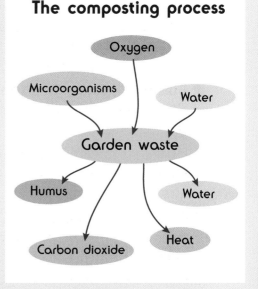

G   Test questions can focus on the way a text is **laid out and organised**, e.g. asking you to comment on or provide text features such as headings and subheadings, or asking you to identify tables, charts and graphs.

11   The best subheading for paragraph 1 of 'How does composting work?' would be:

A ☐ What is composting?

B ☐ Why compost?

C ☐ Natural processes

D ☐ Breaking matter down

12   Why did the author decide to start a new paragraph at line 11?

A ☐ Because the subject has changed and the author is no longer talking about how composting works.

B ☐ Because the author is about to give information on what you need to make composting work.

C ☐ Because the author wants to break up the text.

D ☐ Because the author is about to begin a series of instructions.

13   The visual information entitled 'The composting process' is presented as:

A ☐ a picture

B ☐ a graph

C ☐ a table

D ☐ a diagram.

Test tip

Questions like Question 11 want you to think about the way the text is broken up into paragraphs, and identify the main point of a paragraph.

You need to understand the differences between tables, graphs, pictures, diagrams and charts.

- A **table** has rows and columns, and contains information in the form of words and/or numbers.
- **Graphs** are used to compare information based on numbers, and show trends.
- **Diagrams** are drawings with labels.
- **Pictures** can be drawings or photos – they do not usually have labels.
- **Charts** are a visual way of presenting information – such as bar graphs and pie charts.

Questions sometimes refer to information as presented in pictorial, graphical, tabular or diagrammatic form (pictorial = picture, graphical = graph, tabular = table, diagrammatic = diagram).

14   Which of the following is <u>not</u> true, according to the visual information entitled 'The composting process'?

A ☐ Water is needed for the composting process to take place.

B ☐ Humus is an outcome of the composting process.

C ☐ You need to add heat to garden waste in order to get compost.

D ☐ Microorganisms are needed for composting to take place.

First read this ...

- When you are asked questions about **word meaning**, look carefully at the meaning of the whole paragraph and then the specific sentence you are working on.

- When you are asked questions about **grammar** in the test, look carefully for agreement between subject and verb in the sentence, and between verb tense and statements about past, present or future. Also look for clear and correct use of pronouns.

- When you are asked about **punctuation**, try reading the sentence aloud in your head. Look carefully for missing inverted commas, question marks and commas.

- When you are asked questions about **spelling**, think carefully about words that sound the same but are spelt differently or about common spelling patterns in words, or unusual spellings.

Now try it!

1   Questions 1–8 are about this draft complaint letter concerning a proposed new shopping development in the town of Spilsbury.

	Dear Sir	line 1
para 1	Further to your leaflet about the Elmers Drive shopping development	line 2
	I will write to give my opinions as requested.	line 3
para 2	As an elderly resident of Elmers Road, _____ concerned at the	line 4
	proximity of the development to the quiet area where many pensioners	line 5
	live. The inclusion of a multiplex cinema shops and other leasure facilities	line 6
	would no doubt increase levels of noise from young people in the area.	line 7
	You will be aware of the recent problems with teenagers causing trouble	line 8
	in the town centre and until there is a higher level of policing in Spilsbury,	line 9
	I think this will _____ more of this kind of behaviour.	line 10
para 3	Whilst it would be good to have more shops in Spilsbury, those that are	line 11
	included in the currant proposals add little to what is already available in	line 12
	the town. I can't understand why they are not being more creative in your	line 13
	suggestions? Were there to be a major department store, I would wholly	line 14
	support the shopping proposal. Is it possible to add this to the plans? The	line 15
	common high-street shops that are currently on your lists, will reduce	line 16
	Spilsbury to yet another anonnimous market town. _____ will, of	line 17
	course, add pressure on the few individual shops in the town that is not	line 18
	part of these large chain stores.	line 19
para 4	I do hope you will consider my proposals. The needs of elderly people	line 20
	living near to the development should be taken fully into account.	line 21
	Yours faithfully	line 22
	Marion Eimons	
	Marion Eimons	

A Questions on **vocabulary** may ask you to:

■ choose another word that means the same thing

■ fill a gap with the best word

■ identify a word that has been used incorrectly.

Questions 1–3 focus on vocabulary.

---

1 The best word to replace 'proximity' on line 5 is:

A ☐ size   B ☐ closeness

C ☐ distance   D ☐ dominance

2 The best word to fill the gap on line 10 would be:

A ☐ encourage   B ☐ advantage

C ☐ limit   D ☐ rise

3 A word has been misused on:

A ☐ line 9   B ☐ line 10

C ☐ line 11   D ☐ line 12

Test tip

When you answer a question that asks you to find the best word to replace a particular word, you need to understand the word's meaning.

■ Read the sentence containing the word very carefully. Ask yourself: *'What does it mean?'*

■ Try to make sense of what the writer is saying.

■ Read the sentences **before** and **after** the sentence you are focusing on too. Then think what the word means.

■ If you are stuck, say the sentence to yourself using each of the alternative words in turn. This may well help.

B Questions on **spelling** may ask you to find where a word has been misspelt or to identify the correct spelling.

---

4 A word has been misspelt on:

A ☐ line 4   B ☐ line 6

C ☐ line 8   D ☐ line 14

5 What is the correct spelling for the word 'anonnimous' on line 17?

A ☐ anonymous   B ☐ annonymus

C ☐ anonimus   D ☐ anonymouse

Test tip

Remember that when the question says 'a word has been misused', you are often looking for a homophone, i.e. a word that sounds like another word. For example, maybe the text uses a word like 'ensure' when it should use 'insure'.

C Questions on **punctuation** may ask you to identify where punctuation has been misused or missed out.

> **6** A comma has been missed out on:
>
> A ☐ line 4   B ☐ line 5
> C ☐ line 6   D ☐ line 7

> **7** There is a punctuation mistake on:
>
> A ☐ line 5   B ☐ line 8
> C ☐ line 11   D ☐ line 14

> **8** A comma has been used wrongly on:
>
> A ☐ line 9   B ☐ line 14
> C ☐ line 16   D ☐ line 17

Test tip

When a question asks you to find a punctuation mistake or a grammatical error without telling you exactly what kind of mistake it is, you need to start by reading all the lines referred to in the possible answers very carefully before deciding which answer is correct.

D Questions on **grammar** may ask you to identify:

- connectives (words that can join two sentences or two parts of the same sentence, e.g. *because* and *or*)
- inconsistency in tense, such as a sentence that begins in the past and moves into the present, e.g. *We were walking down the road when we see Mark.*
- places where the subject and verb of a sentence do not agree, e.g. *The children comes round every evening.*
- pronouns that have been used wrongly, e.g. *The boy put on their socks.*

Questions 9–14 give examples of some of the main types of questions on grammar.

> **9** The most suitable word to join together the two sentences on lines 20–21 is:
>
> A ☐ and   B ☐ although
> C ☐ but   D ☐ because

> **10** Which words would best fill the gap on line 4?
>
> A ☐ we are   B ☐ she is
> C ☐ I am   D ☐ they are

11 Which of these lines contains a verb in the wrong tense?

A ☐ line 3   B ☐ line 6
D ☐ line 10   E ☐ line 12

12 Which of the following lines contains a grammatical error?

A ☐ line 11   B ☐ line 14
C ☐ line 18   D ☐ line 20

13 Which of these lines contains a pronoun that has been wrongly used?

A ☐ line 7   B ☐ line 13
C ☐ line 14   D ☐ line 20

14 Which pronoun would best fill the gap on line 17?

A ☐ I   B ☐ We
C ☐ They   D ☐ He

Track your progress

Write the date when you completed each unit, and tick to show whether you'd like more practice or whether you're happy with your skills in each unit. Don't forget to add your score from the end of section tests, and add up your total score at the end!

Section A: Reading for information and understanding					
Unit	Skills covered	Date	I'd like more practice with this	I'm OK with this	End of section test score
1	Skimming, scanning and close reading of texts				
2	Understanding difficult words in a text				
3	Finding the main points and details in a paragraph, section or whole text				
4	All Section A skills				/6

Section B: Understanding the features of different texts					
Unit	Skills covered	Date	I'd like more practice with this	I'm OK with this	End of section test score
1	How information texts are organised				
2	Understanding tables with words and symbols				
3	Understanding tables with words and numbers				
4	All Section B skills				/6

Section C: Understanding how writers achieve their purpose					
Unit	Skills covered	Date	I'd like more practice with this	I'm OK with this	End of section test score
1	Identifying audience and purpose				
2	Understanding the features and language of description texts				
3	Understanding the features and language of explanation texts				
4	Understanding the features and language of persuasive texts				
5	Understanding argument texts and identifying points of view				
6	Understanding the differences between formal and informal texts				
7	All Section C skills				/6

Section D: Spelling words correctly

Unit	Skills covered	Date	I'd like more practice with this	I'm OK with this	End of section test score
1	Spelling strategies				
2	Making words plural, and exceptions to the rules				
3	Spelling words that sounds the same				
4	Suffixes and double letters				
5	All Section D skills				/8

Section E: Punctuation

Unit	Skills covered	Date	I'd like more practice with this	I'm OK with this	End of section test score
1	How to write complete sentences using correct punctuation				
2	How to use commas correctly				
3	Rules for using apostrophes correctly				
4	How to deal with apostrophes on words that end in s and plurals				
5	How to use inverted commas to show quotations, titles and other special uses of language				
6	How to organise text into paragraphs				
7	All Section E skills				/8

Section F: Grammar

Unit	Skills covered	Date	I'd like more practice with this	I'm OK with this	End of section test score
1	Connecting parts of sentences together				
2	Choosing the right tense for verbs				
3	Making sure that the subject and verb agree				
4	Using pronouns to make meaning clear				
5	All Section F skills				/7

Section G: Preparing for the test

1	Working out what a question is asking you to do				
2	How to answer questions on meaning, grammar, punctuation and spelling				

Add up your total score from all the end-of-section tests here:	/41

If you got more than 28/41, congratulations! This shows that you're doing well with most of the skills tested in the Adult Literacy test.

If you got less than 28/41, don't worry – look again at the sections you found difficult and do the related practice sheets from the Teacher's Handbook.

Published by:
Edexcel Limited
One90 High Holborn
London
WC1V 7BH
www.edexcel.org.uk

Distributed by:
Pearson Education Limited
Edinburgh Gate
Harlow
Essex
CM20 2JE
www.longman.co.uk

First published 2006

ISBN   1-84690-134-0
       978-1-84690-134-8

Edited and typeset by Ken Vail Graphic Design
Cover and text design by Ken Vail Graphic Design
Cover image courtesy of Photos.com
Printed and bound in Great Britain by Scotprint, Haddington
The publisher's policy is to use paper manufactured from sustainable forests.

◎ Hot Topics CD
This CD was produced as part of the DfES Move On project 2003–6 and carries Crown copyright. Details of the Move On project and its successor Move On Up, commissioned by QIA, can be found at www.move-on.org.uk.

Acknowledgements
We are grateful to the following for permission to reproduce copyright material:
p5 *New England Spin Doctor* from www.thenewspaper.org.uk, reprinted with permission; p7 *Real-life star's World Cup ambitions* from www.thenewspaper.org.uk, reprinted with permission; photograph of Eniola Aluko courtesy of The Football Association; p10 *Dealing with emergencies* from www.fireservice.co.uk; p12 extract and photograph of Billy Higgins from www.kugb.org and www.sei-do-kan-karate.co.uk, reprinted with permission; p15 extract on Rastafarianism from www.uri.org © 2002 United Religions Initiative; p17 *Swapping a paperclip for a House!* from First News, 14–20 July 2006, reprinted with permission; p20 extract from PEMBROKESHIRE: A BREATH OF FRESH AIR produced by Pembrokeshire County Council, reprinted with the kind permission of Pembrokeshire County Council; p22 *The road to gold starts here: Birmingham 2007 European Athletics Indoor Championships* reprinted with permission; photograph © Mark Shearman, official photographer for UK Athletics; p28 The Prince's Trust leaflet get out of your box copyright © The Prince's Trust, reprinted with permission; p30 extract from RAILWAY TIES by Morrie Erickson: this excerpt first appeared in Salon.com, at http://www.salon.com and an online version remains in the Salon Archives, reprinted with permission; p32 extract and photograph from Letitia Hardy's diary of a year doing voluntary work, found at www.travellersworldwide.com/peripherals/diary.htm, reprinted with the kind permission of the author; p35 *How Tattoos Work* by Tracey V Wilson, reprinted courtesy of HowStuffWorks.com; p36 page from website of Thames Valley Police reprinted with permission; p44 extract from www.forestonline.org reprinted with permission; p49 extract from *The River Cottage Meat Book* by Hugh Fearnley-Whittingstill, published by Hodder & Stoughton; p88 *How does composting Work?* reprinted with the kind permission of Worcestershire Council.

Photographs
p.4 Alamy/Christopher Hill Photographic; p.5 Empics; p.7 Empics; p.8/9 Alamy/ Profmedia; p.11 Stock.xchng; p.12 Courtesy of Billy Higgins; p.15 Empics; p.16 Corbis; p.18 Stock. xchng; p.21 Stock.xchng; p.26 Roger Scruton; p.30 Corbis; p.32 Letitia Hardy; p.43 Photos.com; p.50 Alamy/Superstock; p.57 Alamy/ nagelstock.com; p.59 istockphoto; p.60 Corbis; p.62 Rex Features; p.63 Alamy/Clare Charleston; p.64 Empics; p.69 Stock.xchng; p.74 Getty-Images; p.75 Stock.xchng; p.79 Photos.com; p.81 Stock.xchng; p.83 Alamy/Photofusion; p.84 Graeme Morris.

Every effort has been made to trace the copyright holders and we apologise in advance for any unintentional omissions. We would be pleased to insert the appropriate acknowledgement in any subsequent edition of this publication.

The publisher would also like to thank all schools involved in the research for this book.